Rescue From
the Dark Side

by

Georgeanne DeWitt

HONOR

Tulsa, Oklahoma

Rescue From the Dark Side
ISBN 0-89274-589-4
(formerly ISBN 0-88144-029-9)
Copyright © 1989 by Georgeanne DeWitt
DeWitt Ministries
P. O. Box 73306
Houston, Texas 77273-3306

Published by Honor Books
P. O. Box 35035
Tulsa, Oklahoma 74153

DEDICATION

This book is lovingly dedicated to Roger, the direct opposite of the main character, Barry. Roger is my husband, childhood sweetheart, pastor, exhorter, lover, and my very best friend.

May God richly bless all who read this book.

— Georgeanne DeWitt

FOREWORD

In this exciting story Georgeanne DeWitt portrays a condition in modern society that needs the immediate attention of the total Church.

Georgeanne dramatically emphasizes the danger of the occult and how one can be snared without realizing it. At this moment millions of people in our society are flowing away from God toward all forms of spiritism, sorcery and witchcraft which produce only sadness and death.

I am sure you will enjoy reading this fascinating story of the power of God to set people free from every darkness of the enemy.

Read it and pass it on to a friend!
— Dr. Lester Sumrall
(Founder, Lester Sumrall Evangelistic Association, LESEA Television Network and World Harvest Bible College; Pastor, Christian Center Cathedral of Praise) South Bend, Indiana

PREFACE

For I would have you know, brethren, that the gospel which was preached by me is not according to man.

For I neither received it from man, nor was I taught it, but I received it through a revelation of Jesus Christ.

Galatians 1:11,12

Like Paul, my husband saw the error of the occult and cultic churches by revelation of the Holy Spirit.

In no way does this book reflect our own testimony or our lives. It is not someone else's testimony. This is a purely fictional book.

Our own personal story began in the 1960's when eastern religions first gained their height of popularity and began to spread their influence into denominational churches. A common saying in that era was, "Many pathways lead to the throne of God." At that time, Roger and I had not yet come to realize the truth of Jesus' admonition that He alone is the way, the truth and the life. We worked our way through a maze of churches, not realizing that man is not saved by works, but by grace and the blood of Jesus. We watched as friends, even pastors, became deeply involved in the world of the occult. Our own involvement consisted of the reading of occultic material, some of which had even become available to us through Christian friends and the church. We also became ensnared by the cunning appeal of Satan.

As my own personal search for truth deepened, my health deteriorated. A doctor reported that I had arthritis. The joints in my legs were inflamed, which caused difficulty in walking. The tear ducts in my eyes dried up, causing pain and blurred vision. My blood sugar fell to an alarmingly low level. One diagnosis claimed that I was over 90% allergic. One doctor, endeavoring to find the cause of an acute allergic attack, once asked me, "Well, have you been outside?" Weakly I admitted that I had merely gone out into the yard.

Our first glimpse of the eternal truth that Jesus still heals today occurred while watching Oral Roberts on television. His teaching on "seed faith" caused my husband to decide to give money to his ministry, believing that the end result would be answers concerning the selling of our home and my health problems.

We moved from San Antonio, Texas, to Houston, knowing that God had placed a call on our lives. A few weeks after our move I was invited to attend a faith-filled prayer meeting. There I was puzzled by the happy faces and the glow on each countenance. A few weeks later I received the precious infilling of the Holy Spirit, and I met Jesus as Savior, Lord, Baptizer and Divine Healer. Three days after my infilling, I was impelled to stand in front of a bookcase that decoratively covered one wall of our den. Gently the Holy Spirit instructed me to rid the shelves of all occultic material.

That is why I understand Paul's words so perfectly as they are expressed in Galatians 1:11,12. I did not receive this knowledge from man. Man did not teach me that the occult was wrong. I received this revelation from Jesus. I became a new creature in Christ, and the old life passed away.

Today I am totally healed and actively engaged

in pastoring a church with my husband. Because of our personal experiences and the wreckage of lives we witnessed along the way, I desired to write a novel that would point people to the ultimate truth, the ultimate reality, Jesus Christ. If you embrace Jesus instead of allowing yourself to be ensnared by the occult — which only and always turns out to be as deadly as playing with vipers — then my efforts will have been amply rewarded.

CONTENTS

But realize this, that in the last days difficult times will come.

For men will be lovers of self, lovers of money, boastful, arrogant, revilers, disobedient to parents, ungrateful, unholy,

unloving, irreconcilable, malicous gossips, without self-control, brutal, haters of good,

treacherous, reckless, conceited, lovers of pleasure rather than lovers of God;

holding to a form of godliness, although they have denied its power; and avoid such men as these.

For among them are those who enter into households and captivate weak women weighed down with sins, led on by various impulses,

always learning and never able to come to the knowledge of the truth.

And just as Jannes and Jambres opposed Moses, so these men also oppose the truth, men of depraved mind, rejected as regards the faith.

But they will not make further progress; for their folly will be obvious to all, as also that of those two came to be.

2 Timothy 3:1-9 NASB

1
INNOCENT TEMPTER

Every Sunday morning it was the same. The entourage of parishioners flowed smoothly into the church and sat in their usual pews, as though someone had assigned them seats. Jeannie didn't know why that irritated her so much, since she usually sat in the same place, too. She decided that whoever had coined the term "creatures of habit" must have been sitting in this church at the time.

Someone tapped her on the shoulder and she turned around, knowing that it would be Loretta saying hello as she did every Sunday morning at five minutes till nine.

Jeannie spotted Barry at the back of the church and she watched him with unrestrained pride as he walked down the center aisle toward the altar, his black robe flowing gracefully. There was a hint of flamboyance in his soft, gentle looks. She smiled and glanced out the window.

She could see the whole suburban neighborhood from where she sat. The view was unimaginative although the church was perched upon a hill. A few old wood-frame houses and sparse scrub oaks held her attention momentarily. The warmth of the sun streaming through the window felt good on her bare arms and she thought happily that the cold weather was hopefully gone for good. She needed to get out in the garden and feel and smell the richness of the earth again. She wondered what kind of flowers she should plant....

A stout man with a stoic expression on his face

stood up in the choir and began to sing in a deep voice. Jeannie didn't know him, but then she didn't know a lot of the people around her, although she and Barry had been at the church almost four months.

She heard Barry's voice and turned her head to watch him again. His soft brown hair and big brown eyes made him look much younger than he really was. His face was at times wide-eyed and innocent, at other times compassionate and worldly-wise. His enthusiastic, almost pleading voice resounded through the building.

It's going to take a lot more than pleading to resurrect this group, she thought glumly. Her thoughts jolted back to happier days in college.

"Two buzzes, Jeannie," her roommate had called from the other room one afternoon. "That means you've got company downstairs. Hope he's good-looking!"

Jeannie had brushed back her long, blonde hair and scrutinized herself in the mirror. Her dark print dress emphasized the slenderness of her body. She wished she could be just two inches shorter; she wanted desperately to be able to look up at people for a change.

A tall man with deep-brown eyes that matched his hair was standing by the fireplace downstairs.

"Hi. I'm Barry Holstedt."

She stared at him blankly, wondering if he had wandered into the wrong dormitory. She was sure she would have remembered him if he had been in any of her classes.

He grinned and walked toward her. "I play golf, I have a degree in social work, I plan to be a minister, and what's more, I plan to marry you."

Jeannie had stared up at him incredulously, then realized that he was serious. Irritated by his conceit and the touch of arrogance in his voice, she had replied, "It seems as though you've planned your life precisely; however, you're sadly mistaken in choosing me as wife material. I have a few plans of my own, and they certainly don't include you."

He grinned broadly.

"I'll never be a minister's wife."

His grin widened even more.

"You'll never find me behind some teapot administering tea and sympathy to docile old ladies."

He kept grinning.

"Someone else, maybe, but not me," she said. She had wished he wasn't so handsome and tall.

They were married in a little chapel on campus a few months later. The Colorado snow was still all over the ground that day, but she hadn't noticed or cared.

" '...that he gave his only begotten Son, that whosoever believeth in him should not perish, but have everlasting life' (John 3:16)." Barry's voice was gentle now as he looked slowly from one member of the congregation to another. Jeannie watched him as he stood at the pulpit, and she wondered why she had never been able to adjust to being a minister's wife. It wasn't a bad life really, yet she had never really been comfortable in that role. But she loved Barry deeply, and had followed him from one church to another, doling out her share of tea and sympathy.

She and Barry had always made friends easily, both within the church and the three neighborhoods in which they had lived. But here at St. Matthews....

She sighed heavily, remembering their first morning at this church. She had stood in the receiving line as one gloved hand after another touched hers.

"We're so glad to have you at St. Matthew's."

"Your sophisticated beauty will be a tribute to the Women's Society."

"Don't forget to tell her about the bake sale on Friday, Agnes."

"The annual bazaar will be held next week, Mrs. Holstedt. You shouldn't miss it."

"Your children are so special. A boy and a girl! So well-mannered, too!"

The women were cordial and friendly, but Jeannie hadn't found anyone who shared her own interests. These were society women, and some of them were vastly aware that their roles as church workers had a direct bearing on their roles in society. Jeannie liked their enthusiasm, but she had found no one she could really identify with — neither at the church nor in the neighborhood in which she lived.

The choir was singing now and Barry was walking down the aisle, shaking hands as he headed toward the back of the church.

A less-than-gentle tug from ten-year-old Charles and a twisting of her skirt by six-year-old Mary reminded Jeannie that the patience of her children was on a short fuse. She took their hands and went to find Barry.

The short ride from the church to the parsonage was tense, as it had been every Sunday since Barry could remember. Jeannie was on edge — he could feel it. Her usual questions came spilling out in a rush as she looked out the window of the car at the rows of look-alike houses: Why did they have to be here of all places? What possible good could Barry obtain, spiritually or intellectually, from the endless meetings? How long would they have to endure the pleasantries, the hypocrisies of people who didn't really care?

Barry interrupted her questions with laughter. "That's my old girl," he said affectionately.

He pulled into the driveway and turned off the ignition. The children jumped out of the car and ran to the front door. Barry walked around to open Jeannie's door and he studied her as she slowly got out. She was wearing a soft, cream-colored dress and she had pulled her hair up casually in a topknot, though a few strands had refused to stay bound and hung loosely down to her shoulders. He thought she looked just as vibrant and young as she had the first time he had seen her walking across that campus with an obvious determination and zest for life. (Had it been 12 years already?) And she had applied that same zeal and determination in her role as wife and mother. But she had also maintained the same stubborn quality in her dislike of her role as a minister's wife.

Out loud he asked, "Don't you think that after 12 years of marriage you could adjust to, or at least yield to my situation?" He was sorry as soon as he said it, but he knew she couldn't go on forever this way. She was just making it harder on herself and on him. He knew she was lonely here, but he hoped every day that she would change her attitude and try harder to make friends.

Jeannie's mood changed quickly as she studied the tired and gentle look on Barry's face that was

17

present even while he admonished her. She knew these were the characteristics about him that thawed people. They had only been at the new church for a short time. The small church would probably be bustling with activity soon and many would come to hear the vibrant young minister. This had always happened before. She decided that things weren't so bad after all.

But as she looked around her at the houses up and down the street, she couldn't help but compare the neighborhood with the church: They were both sterile and empty. There was some evidence that people resided in the look-alike houses: newspapers were thrown carelessly on the lawns, milk cartons disappeared from their strategic positions around 10 A.M., and an occasional salesman wandered down the street, hoping for some response.

But as she observed the closed doors, the drawn shades, and especially the closed minds and hearts of the community, much of her zeal diminished in the face of the inevitable course her life was taking. As loneliness crept into her life, much of her old zest for life was dying.

Mary, a stereotype of her mother, and just as serious and sensitive, was aware of her mother's loneliness. Her mother needed a friend, and after much searching she had found one for her.

She burst into the house one afternoon and ran to Jeannie.

"Mommy, meet my new friend," she said proudly. A little girl about seven walked in shyly. Her hair hung in long braids and she was wearing a Brownie uniform. "Her mommy is going to be your friend," Mary added.

After a hasty knock at the door, the mother of Mary's new friend entered before Jeannie had time to contemplate her arrival. Blissfully unaware of weather conditions, she stood soaking wet in the hallway. Though nothing in her features spelled beauty, she had a quality about her which Jeannie found almost exotic. Her faded blue jeans were enhanced by a red and green plaid shirt, her black hair was cropped short and she was barefoot. Unaccustomed to bothering with preliminaries, she simply said, "I'm Judy," and walked over to a chair and sat down, surveying her surroundings.

"Jeannie," she said, "I like the vibrations in this house. I felt an instant warmth when I walked in the front door. The color scheme, the paintings, and even the pattern in your curtains have a harmonious quality about them." She looked at Jeannie. "I can sense that you're tense and bored."

Jeannie could think of nothing to say. It had been so long since she had talked small talk with another woman. She ached for a friend for so long and now that someone was finally offering her friendship, she couldn't think of one thing to say! Judy didn't seem to notice, however, but continued chatting in her direct way. She talked about the children and her husband's job. She paused every few minutes to walk across the room and study a painting intently, and she lavished Jeannie with praise and admiration when she noticed Jeannie's signature at the bottom of each of the paintings.

After she left, Jeannie decided that she did like her, despite her odd ways. She liked her straightforward manner, her daring to be different. She spent a restless night dreaming about Judy. She wondered why she felt that their meeting was not accidental.

"This is My commandment, that you love one another, just as I have loved you."

John 15:12 NASB

2
ANGEL OR MAN?

There was an unusual tenseness in the congregation the next Sunday morning, yet Barry spoke with his usual enthusiasm. He talked about social concerns and current interests. He had made tremendous strides in working with young boys who had been outcasts due to social pressures. Jeannie reflected once again that he had missed his calling. He was pouring his life into a soil that seemed incapable of producing crops. She was sure that the congregation just wasn't grasping what he was trying to get across to them.

Her reverie was broken by the whispers of the ladies in back of her.

"Look at his clothes."

"It's obvious that he doesn't come from *our* neighborhood!"

Since a general stir seemed to be focused on the back of the church, Jeannie turned to look. The ladies weren't talking about Barry.

An old man in tattered clothes had entered the church. Some eyes surveyed him with shock, others with indifference. He wedged in between two people on the back row. One red-faced man moved to another seat.

The old man wore a brown leather jacket; one pocket exhibited a prominent hole. Jeannie could see that his shoes were very worn. His face was lined with age — it was leathery, as though he spent a lot of time outside. He had a beard. Her eyes caught his for a moment, and she felt a wonderful peace. His gaze was soft; his eyes reflected warmth and kindness.

Jeannie turned back to look at Barry, who was still preaching enthusiastically at the front of the church, but her mind wandered, and she remembered reading a story about a rich man and a poor man who had both entered a church. The rich man had been given the best seat in the house, and the poor man had been asked to stand or to sit on the floor.

She turned to look at the old man again, but he was gone.

He who gives attention to the word shall find good,
and blessed is he who trusts in the Lord.

Proverbs 16:20 NASB

3
SETTING A TRAP

"I just made a fresh pot of coffee," Jeannie said, taking two cups and saucers from the cabinet.

"A good cup of coffee stimulates conversation," Judy said. "Which reminds me, I brought a few books with me that I think might interest you. You're a very deep person, Jeannie, and it's obvious that you're searching for truth, the ultimate truth about life. Am I right?"

Jeannie sipped her coffee slowly. "I guess so. You know, Judy, I love Barry and I've been greatly influenced by him. His beliefs are simple, yet he has a commitment, a goal. To pursue his goal is truth for him. He talks about the life of Jesus and uses His life as an example for social reforms. I believe that Jesus existed, but I can't seem to find Him in this cluttered, selfish world."

"You're much too intelligent to be caught up in a fairy tale existence, Jeannie. Forgive me if I sound overly critical, but look at the church you're in. It isn't capable of producing a miracle! If Jesus Christ walked in next Sunday they would vote Him down socially. You're right, your husband is simplistic, but life is not simplistic! You need to find out what your past activities were and then you can solve whatever problems you have right now."

"What do you mean, past activities?"

"I'll be right back," Judy said. She left the room. Jeannie stood up and began to water the plants on the bay window sill. The room was cheerful. Sunshine flooded through the window, and Jeannie could see her flowers beginning to push through the soil in the garden outside.

Judy returned with a paper bag and began placing books on the dining room table. "Here," she said, "I brought a few of the books with me. Some are about reincarnation; others are about the occult in general. I think these should help to answer some of your questions, and there are plenty more where these came from."

Barry sat behind his crowded desk. He had a heavy schedule that day. So many people needed help with mental health problems, marital and spiritual. He had ten minutes to relax before Loretta Gardner would arrive for counseling. He wondered how the rest of the world was faring if church people had so many problems. Didn't anyone have a stable marriage? He thought again how Jeannie had never adjusted to being a minister's wife.

He stood up and began to pace up and down the room. Occasionally he would stiffen and clench his fists. He had felt the incredible tenseness for a long time, but the last three weeks had been especially trying on his nerves. He often felt that he would break if just one more person approached him with a problem. He just couldn't seem to recapture the buoyancy he had once known. It was slipping away from him and he knew that something vital was missing, something that had been there before during every waking moment. Maybe Jeannie was right. He had goals, but the direction was becoming vague. He sighed and sat down, staring at the pile of papers on his desk. He felt like he was walking alone through a dark tunnel and no light welcomed him at the other end.

After a zesty knock at the door, Loretta bustled in and took her usual position in the chair facing his desk. She was middle-aged and plump; her gray and blue flowered house dress made her look completely shapeless. She was the church's most faithful worker. Actually, Barry had encouraged this, thinking that if she were busy she wouldn't have time to center on all of her neuroses. Her most recent project was puppet-making, and she had every member of the Women's Society heartily involved.

He sensed that something was different about Loretta today, then realized that she was completely alone. She usually had a menagerie of children following her. She was the mother of seven.

"How are you feeling today, Loretta?" he asked.

"I feel another one of my nervous headaches coming on." She rubbed her forehead. "Jerry swallowed one of the puppets' eyes last week and my husband wasn't around to help. He's only home long enough to remind me that my whole wardrobe is composed of maternity clothes."

"Remember our conversation last week? What did you do about your hostilities?"

Loretta was frowning and looking down at her dress, trying unsuccessfully to smooth out the wrinkles with her hands. "As soon as I get rid of one hostility, another crops up, thanks to the creativity of my children." She sighed heavily.

Give me strength, Barry thought. Out loud he said, "How many activities are you involved in right now?"

"Well, I'm a Sunday School teacher, youth leader, puppet coordinator, choir director, P.T.A. president, and a Boy Scout leader. Oh yeah, and at last count, I was the mother of seven. Or is it eight now?"

This woman definitely needs to go home and clean her house, Barry thought with amusement. *But just think how many replacements I'd have to get for her!*

They talked for a while about the upcoming church picnic, and Barry talked her into letting someone else take over the preparations for the annual event.

As Loretta departed, somewhat happier now that she had shared her burdens with her pastor, Barry reached for an aspirin. Every encounter with her type drained him more, and he got ready to counsel with several more like her. His major in psychology and degree in social work were of little help now. Why couldn't he reach these people? What was the key? He decided the reason for his fatigue and listlessness must be spring fever. It sneaked up on him every year while he wasn't looking. He sighed and picked up a pile of papers.

The four preschoolers awaited Loretta in the car. Most of their life was spent waiting in the car while she kept her busy schedule.

"Next stop: Jeannie Holstedt's," Loretta said as she climbed into the car. "I know the poor girl needs cheering up. Michael, put your shoes back on. Jerry, quit pulling Lucy's hair. Loretta, stop having kids."

Loretta found Jeannie in a very pensive mood. She had finished reading several of the books that Judy had given her, and they had really captured her imagination, especially when the theory of reincarnation had been introduced in some of them. The books had carefully explained that reincarnation was not to be confused with transmigration of souls. It would be perfectly ridiculous, the authors had said, for a person to return in another life as the family dog or cat.

In the theory of reincarnation, they said, a person might live several lifetimes to purify and perfect his soul. Would God allow one person to be born crippled and blind, and place another person in a rich home, beautiful and healthy, without some sort of recompense? Was that the way a loving God would handle things? No, they said. There had to be a sense of justice in the whole scheme of things. The books stressed that a person might have learned perseverance in his life as a sea captain, but if he had failed to root out bitterness, he would have to return in another lifetime to overcome that bitterness.

Each lifetime that a person gained greater perfection, he reached a different plane until finally he reached Almighty God. Only a few had reached a level of purity to see Him.

"What do you think about the possibility of reincarnation, Loretta?" Jeannie asked her.

"I'm not sure. I've never given it much thought. It seems like if we had to work so hard to gain perfection and reach some level of purity, why would Jesus have died on the cross as an act of love to bridge the gap between man and God? The whole theory seems to me to deny the concept of Christ as Savior."

"But these books talk more about Jesus than the church does, Loretta! Every chapter begins with a scripture explaining its meaning. The Sunday School teacher spends time every Sunday disproving the Bible, at least it seems that way to me sometimes. He leads me to believe that many of the events illustrated in the Old Testament are invalid and mythical. I was refreshed to read something supporting biblical views! I've always had so many doubts.''

''I remember now!'' Loretta exclaimed, jumping up. ''I was motherless in my last life!''

Jeannie laughed and pitched a pillow on the floor and lay down to assume a more comfortable position. Her long blonde hair draped on the pillow. People were usually drawn to Jeannie, because she harbored no pretense. She used her hands when she talked, clutching them to her chest when she was talking about something serious, waving them around when she was excited. Now her face assumed a more serious expression as she endeavored to tell Loretta something that had been bothering her all day.

''Let me tell you about the dream I had last night,'' she said. ''I dreamed that I was a pioneer woman. I lived with my minister husband and four children in a log cabin. The winter was hard and cold. We had very little to eat. Sometimes a neighbor would bring us food, but it was rare even seeing people. My resentment grew when I saw myself in the dream sewing pieces of old clothing together to make new outfits for my family. The resentment was so strong that I woke up angry. I have two tremendous hangups in life, Loretta — I abhor sewing and being a minister's wife! Now doesn't that dream seem a little significant?''

Loretta laughed. ''I think you just ate too much before you went to bed, Jeannie! You sure do take the dullness out of life.'' She suddenly looked serious.

''There are a couple of things that I've wondered about though, since we're on the subject of... well, whatever you call it. Psychic phenomena, I guess it's called. I watched a talk show the other night about poltergeist ghosts. They're ghosts who like to play jokes on people. Several of the people on the panel claimed that ghosts inhabited their houses. It reminded me of an experience I had when I was about ten years old that I've never shared with anyone. As I was getting ready for bed one night, I looked up and saw a small-framed man walking toward me. I sat up in bed with my eyes wide open and watched him approach me. He had a ridiculous smile on his face. I watched him disappear into thin air! I rushed to tell my parents, but they dismissed it as my imagination. And there were other weird things. Sitting near a certain chair in our living room, we would often hear a bell ring at five in the evening. Later we learned that our house had been built on the site of a factory. The factory men used to be dismissed from work at that time every evening!''

Loretta shivered. She had remembered those experiences many times, but had never voiced them until now.

''There, that's what I mean. I really believe that these things exist, Loretta, and I want to find out more about them. I've had a couple of experiences in my life that I consider to be of a psychic nature too. My grandfather died when I was quite small, and I was told that he had gone on a trip. I remember how diligently I searched for him the day he died. I was sure that he wouldn't leave me. We had been pals for so long.'' Jeannie paused for a minute, then continued, a faraway look on her face.

"I was playing in the back yard one afternoon, and I saw him very distinctly. I can still see his snow-white hair, his small mustache, and his twinkly blue eyes as he stood in front of me that day. I ran to him and said hello, and I had a strong impression that he was trying to tell me not to worry, that he was okay. I only saw him for a few seconds, but since then I've always felt that he has been with me, protecting and guiding me through life.

"Another time when I was around the age of ten, these three beautiful ladies sort of floated towards me. I know it must sound funny but it really happened. Anyway, one of them didn't look like the lady I remembered as my grandmother, yet I was sure it was her. She was old, wispy, and continually busy. I felt like she too was letting me know that she had her eye on me, and that she would watch over me."

They sat in silence for a moment, then Loretta stood up.

"You've really given me a lot to think about, Jeannie." She looked at her watch. "I hate to leave, but I must collect my kids and find the nearest hamburger stand. Don's going to be late again tonight. I want to talk about this again soon. It fascinates me."

Jeannie stood in the doorway amusedly watching Loretta's earnest attempt to leave. Little Jerry was hanging precariously on the third branch of the chinaberry tree. Michael returned several times to collect fallen rocks and special treasures that he had accumulated on the two-hour visit. Lucy ran, both chubby arms stretched out, in a direction opposite Loretta's destination. Paul, the quiet one, was finally found in a corner of the guest room reading a book. Finally the car started and many little hands waved good-bye to Jeannie.

Trust in the Lord with all your heart, and do not lean on your own understanding.

Proverbs 3:5 NASB

4
WEAVING A WEB

Jeannie surveyed her house with a critical eye, then hurriedly picked it up, thawed a couple of steaks, chilled a bottle of wine, and took a quick bath. She took the children to a neighbor's house, lit some candles, and prepared to spend a quiet night alone with her husband. She wanted him all to herself for a change.

But Barry's mood that evening did not exude romance. He had seemed rather distant lately, almost aloof. Jeannie reprimanded herself on her own silent mood. She knew she was self-centered. She also knew that her ways had become nagging and critical. She had been more concerned with her own problems and needs than her husband's. As she looked at his tired face, she resolved that from now she would endure with more cheerfulness the endless boring meetings she was required to attend. Remembering the reincarnation philosophy she had read about, she shuddered at the possibility of finding herself in the same situation, life after life, until she adjusted to whatever it was that she was supposed to adjust to.

That evening after she had given Barry time to rest, she walked into the living room. Barry had a book open in his lap but he was staring into the fireplace. He looked exhausted and Jeannie suddenly thought he looked older. He looked up at her and held out his arms.

She sat on his lap. "Can you tell me about it?" she asked.

"Darling, lately life seems so empty. I knew what my goals were once, but somewhere along the line I seem to have lost sight of them. All day I counsel with people, and a week later they're back in my office with more of the same problems. I wish I could just write a prescription for them, or give them a handy antidote to end all their stress. Quite honestly I think I feel as hard-pressed as they do."

Jeannie rested her head on his shoulder. "Barry, I think this might be a good time for me to tell you about my friendship with Judy, and some of her ideas about life.'

She related her story and found to her amazement that her sophisticated husband registered little surprise and was listening very attentively.

"Those are interesting ideas," he said. "I've been drawn to the theory of reincarnation for some time now. Maybe these things go along with the Bible, and maybe we've missed the boat by not finding out more about them. Christ did say that we must be born again. That may support reincarnation theories to some extent."

Jeannie nodded vigorously. "That's exactly what some of those books brought out. And Judy thinks we could find out why we're having the problems we're having right now if we knew something about our former lives — if reincarnation is a reality, of course. If we found out it wasn't we would have lost nothing."

"You know," Barry said thoughtfully, "I've thought a lot about astrology lately, too. I've been reading up on it a little. It's really fascinating. But we can't dive into all of this headfirst. It's important that we remember that some of these theories neglect to keep God as their central force.''

''Listen Barry, Judy told me how much group therapy has helped her. It gives people a chance to be open and honest with each other. And you know me, I've always felt that honesty is the greatest virtue in a person. Most of the people around us are so closed. Just think of the potential. Would you consider leading couples in a few group sessions?''

He looked at her excited face affectionately, then put his arms around her. ''You remind me of my old girl tonight. You know, I think with you by my side, anything is possible.''

He kissed her forehead, then her nose. ''Let's go get those steaks,'' he said. ''I'm suddenly starved.''

They walked to the kitchen arm in arm.

Our soul waits for the Lord; He is our help and our shield.

Psalm 33:20 NASB

5
ANGELS IN CHARGE

Jeannie tried to approach morning as tenderly as possible. She woke an hour before the rest of the family and sneaked into the kitchen. The coffee perked busily as she arranged the juice, bacon, eggs, and hot biscuits artistically on the table. The sun flooded through the dining room window. She wanted just one quick cup of coffee before she woke them.

"Mommy, can I take my butterfly net with me to catch frogs today?"

She whirled around startled, and saw Charles perched upon the barstool.

"How long have you been sitting there, Charles?"

"Oh, awhile. Can I Mommy? Please?"

"I don't see why not. Are you excited about the picnic?"

He grinned. "Yeah! Daddy says I can eat all I want. Can I?"

"You sure can, little one. Will you go wake up Daddy and Mary for me?"

Mary walked in carrying her doll. Dressed in a lace pink robe and pink slippers, she looked the picture of femininity. Her long blonde hair made her look much like her mother, but she had Barry's big brown eyes. She was a quiet little girl, unlike her brother who voiced every thought and desire to anyone who would listen.

"It's going to be fun swimming at the picnic today," she said as she placed her doll in its tiny high chair beside the table.

"How's my family?" shouted Barry with a gusto that made them all jump. He walked briskly into the kitchen and lovingly ruffled Mary's hair.

"Hi yourself!" Jeannie said. *At least he seems more himself,* she thought as she walked over and hugged him.

It was the day of the annual church picnic and Barry and Jeannie were also celebrating their six-month anniversary at the church. The children ran around excitedly while Jeannie fried two chickens.

The drive to the picnic wound through hills, and the children's anticipation mounted when the car reached its highest point on a hill. They got out of the car for a moment to see the breathtaking view. They were entranced by the lushness of the valley, green and fertile, with its large oak trees spreading their protection over the picnic tables scattered here and there along the river. They could see the river meandering through the greens, blues, and browns that framed the forest.

Jeannie and Barry held hands and breathed in the freshness of nature. Jeannie studied the look on Barry's face. He looked peaceful for a change, although still somewhat drawn and tired. They climbed back in the car and drove down to the valley where other picnickers would soon arrive and spread their mouth-watering dinners under the trees.

Charles could picture the golden-fried chicken, the hot rolls and buttered corn-on-the-cob, and the cobblers, cakes, and pies. He thought happily that this would be a day he wouldn't soon forget. He loved to eat more than anything else in the world.

The stream was spring-fed and clear. Here and there a large rock jutted out of the water and seemed to challenge a visitor to sit on its ample surface.

"I want to lie on that one over there," said Jeannie, pointing to a large gray rock. "I want to soak up the sun like a giant lizard. Did you ever consider how wise the woodland creatures are?" she asked the children. "They are never anxious. They enjoy the simplicities of life."

People began to arrive and scattered in different directions. The children asked for time to explore and swim before eating, and Jeannie told them to stay within eyesight.

Jeannie and Barry waded out to the rock. The rhythmic sound of the water splashing over the smaller rocks soon made the two of them drowsy.

"Mmmm, this is so nice," Jeannie said lazily, as she lay back on the rock, dipping her feet in the water. "Remember how we used to go to the ocean every weekend when you were working at St. Paul's?"

Barry didn't answer. She looked over at him and saw that his eyes were closed. He was so tired and frustrated and she wished she could take some of his burdens upon herself. She glanced over at the children. They were laughing and splashing each other, and she could see Loretta's kids running down the hill toward the lake.

She closed her eyes and remembered the days when Mary was a baby. They had spent countless afternoons like this at the beach. Barry had never seemed to run out of energy in those days. They had

Bible studies several times a week in their home, and Jeannie was organizing women's prayer groups and counseling young girls in the church. Barry never seemed to have bad days then. Whenever things went wrong, he and Jeannie would pray together and ask God to take away the hurt.

Jeannie smiled, remembering a day when Charles, who was just six then, had come running into the house, sobbing loudly. When he had stopped crying enough to talk, Barry asked him what was wrong.

"The kids in my class laughed at me 'cause I forgot my ABC's," Charles said tearfully.

Barry had scooped him up in his lap and told him "Okay, son. Here's what you do. You close your eyes real tight and think about Jesus and how much He loves you. Then you ask Jesus to put a great big giant band-aid on your heart where it hurts, okay?"

Charles had nodded, then giggled, "Just like the one on my finger where I hurt it."

"Yep," Barry said. "Just like that one."

"Only bigger," said Charles.

"Bigger," said Barry.

Jeannie began to doze off.

Charles was supervising his little sister. He was an excellent swimmer, thanks to Barry. He had made sure Mary stayed on the shallow side of the dam.

Mary had an imaginary playmate, a ladybug named Samantha. Jeannie had invented her in storytelling. Mary held a piece of bark in front of Samantha.

"Would you like to go riding on this nice boat?" she asked Samantha. Receiving her approval, she placed her gently in her boat. Mary walked along with the boat's slow pace, then began to wade into deeper water as the small boat picked up speed with the current.

"Samantha Ann Ladybug! Come back!" she yelled, but the tiny boat had already disappeared around a curve in the river.

The rocks on the bottom of the river bed were sharp, and her feet began to hurt and bleed. The current was pulling her down. By the time Charles spotted her, she had reached the bend.

The river, which was deep at this point, was muddy and brown where Mary was trying desperately to regain her footing.

Charles saw his little sister struggling, and dived in after her.

Mary was hysterical when he reached her. "Just hold on to me and be still," he cried. But she continued to fight the water and her rescuer. The current pulled both of them under.

Loretta's son Jerry was the messenger appointed to warn Barry and Jeannie. He ran with amazing speed through the woods.

Charles felt the warm sun on his face and opened his eyes. The woods looked hazy, but he could see the small figure of his sister lying beside him. He tried to focus on the broad, kind face bending over him, but he could not see the features clearly. The man's large hands were gentle, though, and his voice was comforting. Charles could see that he wore a brown jacket, and that a button was missing from the jacket and the pocket was torn.

Breathless and frightened, Barry and Jeannie ran up on the scene. The stranger was gone. A small, brown piece of bark lay glistening in the sun beside Mary.

Test yourselves to see if you are in the faith; examine yourselves!

2 Corinthians 13:5 NASB

6

EXPLOSIVE TOYS FOR GROWNUPS

Judy appeared early the next morning. Her attire had changed little since her last visit. She was wearing a white shirt with her blue jeans this time, but she hadn't located shoes yet.

Jeannie was glad to see someone who was not only stimulating company but enlightened as well. She told Judy about the picnic and the mysterious stranger who had saved her children.

"Barry questioned some fishermen in a nearby boat. No one had seen an old man."

Judy shrugged and accepted the news in her matter-of-fact way.

"That's not surprising," she said. "I've heard countless stories like that. There's a whole invisible world right at our fingertips, which, by the way, is why I've honored you with such an early morning visit. I thought you might enjoy a ride in the country. It's time you met Carolyn. She has psychic powers and she gives readings to people about their lives."

Jeannie raised her eyebrows, but Judy continued.

"She has helped me tremendously, Jeannie. She said that I have a deep need for fulfillment through creative writing. She gave me the self-confidence to write and the assurance that I would succeed. She also warns people about pursuing career talents that would be detrimental to their spiritual progress.''

"I think you had better elaborate on that one, I haven't read about that yet."

"Well, for instance, this one lady sought Carolyn's advice. She had a beautiful singing voice. She might have been famous had she gone in that direction.''

"And I suppose you're going to tell me that this Carolyn advised her not to pursue a singing career?''

"Precisely,'' Judy said. "In past life experiences, she had been very famous. Carolyn hesitated to tell her who she had been before, since her problem was pride, and pride is what was limiting her spiritual growth in the first place. Carolyn advised her to use her singing talent in churches or in fundraising organizations. She also told her not to accept any money for her services.''

"That's interesting,'' Jeannie said. "I have to admit that I've been really intrigued by all of this, these books and everything. But experimentation is something else. I don't care to climb out on a limb, especially without Barry's approval. I may not be ready to face some of the things your friend might present.''

"Maybe you'd just like to meet her, then.'' Judy smiled, "Believe me, it would be a terrible waste not to take advantage of her talent.'' Jeannie's mind rested, knowing that the children were safe in school.

The drive through the country was peaceful, and Jeannie's imagination soared as she pictured this mysterious Carolyn. She smiled to herself as she pictured an old, snaggled-toothed woman with long, bony fingers, peering into a crystal ball.

The car swirled into the driveway of a rather

unkempt yard. Giant oaks loomed in heavy sequence along the driveway. The two-story house needed painting, but it had an alluring quality about it. The front porch was long, and it was enhanced by three wicker chairs and an old swing that swayed gently in the breeze as though it were occupied.

"Does the whole environment have to be so weird?" Jeannie asked, staring at the moving swing. "This place reminds me of a Hitchcock horror movie!"

Judy laughed heartily. "You and Carolyn will be instant friends. I can just feel it."

The door opened before they had an opportunity to knock. Carolyn stood in the doorway, surrounded by an aura of coolness.

"I've been expecting you," she said flatly.

"Oh, I didn't know Judy called you," Jeannie said.

"She didn't," Carloyn said stiffly, and offered no further explanation.

Jeannie looked at Judy questioningly, and Judy smiled and followed Carolyn into the house.

The meeting was similar to Jeannie's first encounter with Judy. No introductions or small-talk preliminaries seemed necessary. They sat down in the living room.

She's really beautiful, thought Jeannie. Carolyn's blue-black hair trailed halfway down her back. She was not endued with natural curl, but her hair framed her face gracefully. Her fair complexion indicated that she did not take full advantage of the available outdoor life. Her eyes were her most unique feature. Jeannie studied them carefully, deciding that she could not distinguish what color or colors they were.

Carolyn served tea on a silver tray. The china was old, in harmony with the furnishings and the house itself.

"This place belonged to my grandmother," said Carolyn as she poured the tea from a silver teapot. "My mother died when I was very small. I remember very little about her. All I have to remember her by is a chest containing some unusual jewelry that she gave me. Some of the emblems on the jewelry are original."

Jeannie noticed the unusual necklace that Carolyn wore. It had the head of a ram with a woman's breasts.

"I lived with my grandmother here until she died two years ago," Carolyn said. "I prefer to keep the environment unchanged. She was always satisfied with life the way it was."

Carolyn studied Jeannie intently, and Jeannie knew she could sense the uneasiness and tension in her. Jeannie shifted position under Carolyn's gaze, and wondered why she felt uncomfortable, almost afraid. She decided that she was just being overly dramatic. She looked at Carolyn, then looked at her teacup.

Yes, she thought. *Why didn't I see it before? Her eyes are green!* She felt an unnerving spiritual presence. Those eyes!

She looked at Carolyn again, and had a foreboding feeling that something or someone else was peering from behind those bright green eyes.

Carolyn's head jerked suddenly as though she were listening to a voice. Jeannie's uneasiness increased as Carolyn appeared to be communicating with an unknown personage.

"Yes," Carolyn said. "What would you have me tell her? Yes. I think that she has been sent to me. Right now?"

Carolyn's gaze focused on Jeannie again as though she had just remembered her presence. She began to talk to Jeannie in short, choppy sentences, and her eyes were fixed sharply on Jeannie's.

"I think I can help you. You and your husband are in a deep quest for truth. It is fortunate that Judy brought you to me. I will be able to guide you into that truth. A deeper walk will be opened to you. A closer bond in your marriage will develop. I will also be able to help many of the people that your husband is concerned about.

"You have been lonely and bored. This will come to an end. Your husband will receive his old effectiveness in his ministry. You will also be rid of the tormenting guilt feelings that you have of being inadequate as a minister's wife."

Jeannie stared at her, unbelieving. *Certainly Judy had told her about these things. Surely that was it.*

Judy disrupted the silence. "Barry and Jeannie were thinking of developing group therapy sessions for people in their church. Would you consider attending some of the meetings when they progress?"

Carolyn didn't answer, but the expression on her face said "of course," or so Jeannie thought. She thought wryly that Carolyn probably already had the meetings marked down on her calendar.

The group meeting was scheduled for Friday night. Jeannie's eagerness mounted with each passing day. She felt that she was embarking on a voyage of new discovery. She couldn't wait to see people unmask themselves and reveal their true identities.

She was repulsed by and yet drawn to this new world. Her encounter with Carolyn had been a shaking experience, but it was also exciting in a way. Judy had assured her that Carolyn was very deep in her spiritual walk. She was an older soul than most people, meaning that she had lived many lifetimes and had accumulated much knowledge and wisdom about life, and the life hereafter. Ever since Jeannie's visit with Carolyn, Jeannie had experienced feelings of unreality about the whole thing. Or was it reality? She wasn't sure.

Lately she had often felt faint, light-headed, and out-of-touch with the world around her. One day while marketing, she hadn't been able to remember where she was for a minute or two.

Her temper had become short too. These moods heightened as she delved deeper into the books Judy had given her. She thought it was possible that these new discoveries were drawing her closer to God. Maybe she was having a deep religious experience, she thought, and God was leading her to a new world, a more stimulating world.

Friday night finally came and the guests began to arrive.

Jeannie had made refreshments and had moved the furniture around so that they could all sit on the floor in a circle. She wanted things to be as comfortable and casual as possible.

The five couples assembled casually on the floor of the den. Barry assumed a prominent place in the middle of the room. Jeannie sat by the fireplace where she could observe everyone unnoticed. She noted with amusement and surprise that Judy was wearing shoes for a change.

Barry began by explaining that the purpose of the group meeting was to get to know each other better and hopefully to solve any problems within the group.

"It doesn't matter who or what you talk about," he said. "The important thing is to draw out all those problems. Let your spouse or friend know what's inside you. And be honest."

He stopped and looked around. "Would anyone like to begin?"

They all looked at each other and smiled, except Betty Small, who sat frowning while she twisted a Kleenex nervously in her hand. She was an attractive woman, but her looks were diminished by her insecure manner. Jeannie had never known anyone with an inferiority complex like Betty's.

"We never communicate," Betty said bitterly, looking at her husband. "We never even talk to each other anymore."

Her husband, John, looked disgustedly at the ceiling. *Here we go again*, he thought. He was a lawyer and a complete cynic about encounter groups such as this one. He hoped fervently that Betty wouldn't end up crying again. She had cried through ten long years of marriage.

"Well I for one wouldn't find it hard to communicate with a husband like you," Pat Miller said impishly. Pat was a small woman with delicate features which not only enhanced her beauty but caused her to seem childlike and dependent. Unfortunately this childlike dependence wasn't always centered on her husband, Jim, who was a doctor.

Jim looked at her hard. He knew he shouldn't have come. He knew that his wife's attempt to patch up their marital differences through an encounter group was futile. He was tired of her constant flirtations, and he knew that a few meetings wouldn't solve anything, especially when half the group was composed of men.

"You never find it difficult to communicate with any man, Pat, let's face it," he said. "You only have communication problems with husbands and children." He laughed derisively.

Jeannie saw Tom glance at his wife, Janet. Neither of them had said a word and she knew they were uncomfortable. She felt pretty uncomfortable too, but she hoped things would start going better. Betty was always complaining and crying, and Pat was well known as a flirter. Jeannie decided that maybe it was best that they were all letting their inhibitions out now so they could get on to some positive, constructive criticism later. Her thoughts were interrupted by Loretta.

"You think you all have problems?" she was asking. "I challenge any of you to live my life and remain sane. How will I ever fit into this group?" she asked no one in particular. "None of you have peanut butter on your face and frogs in your pockets!"

No one laughed.

Jim turned to Barry suddenly. "Okay, here's a bit of honesty for you, since that's why we're all here. Barry, you can preach for an hour with the most flowery prose I've ever heard and I swear you say absolutely nothing!"

"He has to say nothing to avoid controversy," John said dryly. "That's the only way you can live with some people."

Judy leaned back on her pillow with an exasperated sigh. "This is giving me a headache," she said. "This has got to be the most moronic and sophomoric discussion I've ever heard in my life. Really, you couldn't top it." She looked up at Jeannie, but Jeannie avoided her eyes.

"Yeah, everybody," Judy's husband said sarcastically, "just listen to my intellectual wife. She's only interested in something if it satisfies her thought pattern or gratifies her spiritually." He looked at Judy disgustedly. "Oh dear intellectual wife, if you would only work at making yourself look more attractive, concentrating on the physical instead of the spiritual, we would have a better marriage. You should see the great-looking outfits and hairdos that the girls in the office parade around in." He sat back, crossing his arms and looking smug.

"You knew I was a rugged individualist when you married me," Judy snapped.

Jeannie cringed in the corner of the room. Whatever problems she and Barry had seemed remote and unimportant compared to all this. Was this what honesty provoked — people attacking each other verbally with no feeling or compassion? She decided that this would be a good time to promote a new trend in the conversation.

"I met an interesting lady this week. She's a psychic. She may visit this group one night and share some of her ideas with us." Noticing Janet and Tom exchanging startled glances, she added, "I know it may sound a little offbeat. But she's really interesting, and I think you'll enjoy some of her philosophies.''

"I've had psychic experiences before," Loretta offered. "I had a frightening experience with the ouija board one time. It frightens me even to tell you about it. It predicted that my father would die in a car wreck on a Friday afternoon at three. I became obsessed with the thought; I would call him around two every Friday and warn him not to leave in his car. That was several years ago and I'm always depressed on Fridays. I've always wondered about the power of the board, because many of its predictions come true. Do your children have a ouija board, Jeannie?''

"Yes, Charles has one in his room," Jeannie said reluctantly. "He got it for his birthday." She hesitated. They were all looking at her. She and Barry hadn't really approved of Charles's having the board. They'd read that it was often used for ill means. She glanced at Barry, but he was whispering something to Tom.

"Just a minute — I'll go get it," she said. She sighed with relief as she walked down the hall to Charles' room. This meeting could use a harmless game to break the tension. Anything would be better than listening to the insults that had been hurled across the room earlier.

She returned and set the board on the floor in front of Loretta.

Loretta said, "Sit directly across from me, Jeannie, and hold your hands over the board very still. Good. Now, ask the board a question.''

"Okay, let's see." Jeannie hated being the first one to try out the board. She felt a little silly. "Will Barry and I have any more children?" she asked.

The pointer spelled the answer on the board as quickly as their eyes could follow:*YES—BOY—IN TWO YEARS.*

The board answered questions quickly and easily as long as Loretta participated, yet it moved slowly for some or not at all when she did not participate. Jeannie experienced a tinge of envy for Loretta's apparent power.

"Have you ever heard of automatic writing?" asked Joe, trying to redeem himself from his earlier blunder. "It operates on the same principle. Invisible entities who have died, perhaps loved ones, supposedly control your hands and write messages from the world beyond. Many people have corresponded with close relatives even after death this way. Some messages aid a person in special business ventures. One man I heard about struck oil after he obeyed the instructions that came from his dead business partner. One lady was told that she was too much like Martha in the Bible. She was instructed to relinquish the role of eternal housekeeper and develop her life with people more. Another lady was influenced by an entity to take up drawing. Evidently she had been a fine artist in a previous lifetime and suddenly felt compelled to have a pencil and sketch pad in front of her again."

Barry looked around the room. He had said nothing since the board had been brought out. The onslaught of accusations and angry words hadn't bothered him as much as he was sure they had Jeannie. Nothing shocked him anymore. He was well-acquainted with Betty's tears and bitterness, Pat's flirtations, and Joe's sharp tongue. He wasn't too interested in ouija boards or automatic writing, but it didn't seem to be doing any harm. At least they were all united in one common project for the first time that night. He looked over at Jeannie. She was lying on the floor, her chin cupped in her hand. She looked like a fascinated child at a magic show. He sat back.

Each person took turns experimenting with the automatic writing technique, and each one failed to see any results. Janet shyly volunteered to try, but she too was unsuccessful. Someone suggested that Loretta try since she had had such success with the ouija board. Beginning to enjoy being in the spotlight, Loretta approached the pen and paper with confidence. Her hand in writing position, she held the pen steady for several minutes. She asked Jeannie to propose a question to which no one in the room could possibly know the answer.

"Okay. My sister is supposed to call tonight at eleven. Ask how Marcie is spending her evening, and Marcie can verify the answer when she calls," Jeannie suggested.

After a few minutes, the room heavy with tension and expectation, Loretta's hand began to scrawl a message shakily.

MARCIE HAVING A QUIET EVENING. SHE IS READING A BOOK ABOUT ANDREW JACKSON — HUSBAND WATCHING THE GAME. GOT KIDS TO BED EARLY.

Everyone except Jim was silent. He voiced great skepticism, saying that it was coincidence that made the automatic writing seem so powerful.

"I'll admit that these experiments are all amateurish, simply cheap magic tricks," said Judy, "but they do work. I'd rather practice E.S.P. and mind control. We could send each other messages and if we concentrated hard enough, our mental suggestion could cause every family on this block to have a sudden craving for ice cream. Then we could watch while all of the cars backed out of their driveways simultaneously."

Everyone laughed.

"That's more interesting than finding out what Marcie did with her evening," John said drolly.

The telephone rang promptly at eleven. After a few minutes of conversation, Jeannie began to question her sister about her evening.

"Oh, our evening has been uneventful and quiet. I snuggled up on the couch to read. I'm a widow during football season, you know. Don has been glued to the game all evening."

"What are you reading?"

"*The President's Lady.* It's a story about Andrew Jackson's wife."

"Where are the children?"

"What's that, Jeannie? I can't hear you."

"I just wondered where the children are," Jeannie said, trying to sound casual.

"They went to bed early."

Jeannie hung up the phone weakly. She had that strange, out-of-touch feeling again. Was Judy correct? Was she stepping into a higher plane? Judy had said that some people were on a mountain and that they could clearly see the ones below them. She certainly was seeing new truths, she thought.

She returned to the den and related the news to the group, then went to the kitchen to fix refreshments. No one was talking when she returned.

As each person departed, he expressed the desire to explore the world of the occult further, with the exception of Barry, who thought it best to reserve his judgment until a later time.

"Come to Me, all who are weary and heavy-laden, and I will give you rest."

Matthew 11:28 NASB

7

THE SNAKE STRIKES

Barry stared at his desk, which was piled high with work. Mrs. Jacobs, his secretary, had left a diversity of memos on his desk.

Mrs. Brooks — sick in Lakewood Hospital.

Loretta called — requests office appointment.

Mrs. Brown resigned as President of Women's Society — seems to be dissension within the group.

Mae Purvis — feelings hurt — you never acknowledged her chocolate pie.

Betty Small — couldn't understand message — was crying.

Helen Lester's teenaged boy ran away.

The furrow on his brow deepened. Endless problems that were never solved paraded before him. As he contemplated which message to answer first, his eyes focused on a striking woman standing in the doorway. Carolyn smiled as though she were an old expected friend. Her smile unnerved him and in an awkward attempt to arrange the things on his desk, his papers scattered in all directions. The playful smile remained on her face and she walked to his desk with her usual calm assurance and held out her hand to him.

"Hello, Reverend Barry Holstedt. I've met your wife and I wanted to meet her eminent husband."

"Do you need help with some problem?"

"As a matter of fact, I don't. I came to help you."

'Well, that certainly is unique.''

"It's a beautiful day," she said. "I can sense that you're tied up in knots. Why don't we take a walk while I reveal the nature of my visit?"

Barry was only vaguely aware of the conversation. He thought she was the most exotic woman he had ever seen, if not the most beautiful. So this was the intriguing Carolyn that Jeannie had chattered about so endlessly. Her eyes had a hypnotic quality about them. Any man would gladly be a loyal subject to them.

He suddenly straightened and shaped his face into its most respectful, ministerial expression. What was he thinking? Could the presence of a mere woman make him forget who he was? Yet her being merely a woman seemed an understatement. Something beyond her obvious beauty and charm compelled him to know more about her.

Gathering a business-like tone of voice he said, "No, I really don't have time to take a walk. Why don't you have a seat and explain how you intend to help me."

She sat down with the grace of a model and continued to stare at him fixedly.

She spoke in a quiet, suggestive tone. "Your wife Jeannie has many unspoken hostilities," she said. "She did not confide in me. I perceived this.

"Some people call me a fortuneteller. Others, unfortunately, call me a witch. I am neither. I am a uniquely talented individual, sensitive to the needs and problems of others. Many people seek my help and advice for a fee. I usually give help free to friends, however. This was the tradition of my mother and my grandmother who were also specially gifted. I rarely seek anyone out but I have felt compassion for you and your wife. If you would like a reading, I will do this free of charge." Noticing his puzzled expression, she added, "A reading will show you and your wife who you were in past lifetimes, and that in turn will give you the insight to cope with your problems better in your present life situation."

The buzzer on Barry's desk rudely interrupted their conversation. His secretary said that Loretta wanted to see him immediately. He felt slightly irritated. Loretta needed to see him immediately several times a week. She depended on his counseling for the minutest problems. Loretta was at the door before he could answer.

"Excuse me, Barry. I know you must be busy, but I must talk to someone." She saw Carolyn and stepped back. "Oh, excuse me. I didn't know you had company." She eyed Carolyn with curiosity and concern.

"That's all right, Loretta," Barry said, standing up. "She's a friend of Jeannie's." Why did he feel as though he'd been caught doing something wrong? "Loretta, may I introduce you to Carolyn?"

"I know about you," said Carolyn with that directness that Barry was finding quite frustrating. "I am afraid, Loretta, that we have both caught the young minister at a most inconvenient time. Perhaps I can assist you with your problem."

"Well," Loretta said, looking at Barry uncertainly, "that's very nice of you, but..."

"Nonsense, you're not imposing on me at all. My car is right outside. I was planning to visit Jeannie. Why don't we talk there?"

Carolyn escorted the bewildered Loretta out the

door. Barry was relieved to see them go, but he was rather concerned that they were going to see Jeannie. He was afraid that Carolyn's condescending and domineering personality might be harmful to his wife. He had a strange feeling that she was moving into their lives, even into their circle of friends.

Jeannie was surprised to see Carolyn and Loretta together. What a strange twosome! One was chic and glamorous even in the most casual dress, the other was dowdy and suppressed. Carolyn revealed the nature of their visit. Jeannie looked at Loretta attentively. They walked into the den and sat down.

They exchanged small talk for a few minutes, and Jeannie brought out her latest painting, a desert scene. It was done purely through her imagination, she said; she'd never really been in the desert.

Jeannie could tell that Loretta wasn't really listening to the conversation. She was nervously arranging the pieces of a torn Kleenex into intricate designs on the arm of the chair.

"Are you all right?" Jeannie asked her.

"I can't go on anymore," Loretta said without looking up. "All of my days are running together. I get up, and children invade me from every direction. Lately, the doorbell rings and I find an extra child there. I just stand there and try to keep from screaming. I tend to endless church and civic functions. The children continue to disobey me while I'm on the phone. Occasionally Don is home, but usually he's gone on a business trip. When he is home, he doesn't give me any attention or discipline the children. I feel as though someone is beating on me — thousands of tiny fists beating and beating on me! Sometimes I sit in the yard to get some peace and quiet, but I find no solace there. There are sounds in my head." She looked up at them. "I'm an old woman. When the day ends, I fall into bed. The next day is the same. Exactly the same." She shook her head slowly. "I'm so tired."

Jeannie's heart went out to her. Loretta was usually so cheerful and funny, though a little high-strung. Her dramatics had once irritated Jeannie, but she had grown quite fond of Loretta. She walked over and put her arms around her.

"Loretta, I've noticed for a long time that you're too involved. You mistreat yourself. Why don't you devote an hour or two of the day to your own needs? Get a babysitter. Take a walk. Take a bubblebath, if that relaxes you. Read a good book or listen to some music."

Carolyn listened to Jeannie's advice in amused silence. This was why they needed her. She knew that she could get to the bottom of Loretta's problem, and taking a nice walk was not the solution.

"The two of you have known each other in other lifetimes," she said softly. "Your past lives have a definite link with each other. The past holds the key that could unlock all your problems." She paused.

"I had a dream about the two of you. The setting was cosmopolitan; the buildings loomed largely. The day was gray with prospective rain. The streets were deserted except for two lonely figures. They were not together. In this dream, I was looking down on the city and its streets much as a scientist would look at white mice in a maze. The two people wandered aimlessly, and I could feel agony and torment in their souls. One carried a small baby."

"That was me!" interrupted Loretta. Jeannie

was glad to see that her sense of humor had not entirely left.

"She was hungry and tired," Carolyn continued. "After many days of searching, she saw another figure approaching her. They recognized each other as they got close and they embraced happily. It was after a war. The world was cold, emotionally and physically. One husband had been killed in the war. The other husband was missing. The two friends found food and shelter together. You see, the two of you have been valuable friends in the past." She stopped and looked at them.

"So how can all that help me now?" asked Loretta.

"It can't, unless we delve deeper to find out what's causing your trauma."

"Too many kids are causing my trauma," Loretta said. Carolyn looked stern, and Loretta added, "I don't mean to be disrespectful, Carolyn. Okay, I'm willing to try anything."

Carolyn turned her head to stare fixedly at the wall in front of her, and seemed to submerge into a trance-like state. Jeannie thought her eyes looked like oceans of greens and blues. Her body became limp, and her voice sounded foreign and unnatural.

"I see a large old house with many rooms. The floors are bare. The furniture is sparse. I see two small girls sharing a room. The two little girls are orphans. Life is dull. The ladies running the orphanage don't really care for the children. It is just a job for them. The children are forced to do many chores.

"I know what the children are thinking. One little girl sees life as a testing ground. She knows instinctively that there is much to learn through pressures and hardships. Everything that happens to her strengthens her character. She understands life's great lesson in this situation. She matures into a kind lady. She gives her children love and attention. She is sensitive to their needs and knows that they need love to be secure.

"The other child becomes bitter and hard. She has many resentments. She decides that she will grab everything that life has to offer. She becomes selfish. She is beautiful and men desire her. She mistrusts and hates them. She uses them for her own purposes. Her children receive no mothering from her. She wants to be the child. She considers her children competition for her."

Carolyn shifted position in the rocking chair. A small shaft of light from the window fell on her. The room was beginning to darken with its welcome to evening. Carolyn's eyes enlarged again and she glared suspensefully at Jeannie and Loretta.

"The child who adjusted was you, Jeannie. You accomplished what you were sent to learn in that lifetime. The child who did not adjust was you, Loretta. You will be in that same situation time and time again until you learn what life has to teach you. You are not being a wife and mother. You must not try to escape this responsibility. Go home and earnestly try to center all of your activities on the home."

She turned to Jeannie.

"As you and Loretta are linked together in past lives, you and I are likewise linked together, Jeannie. I will reveal the nature of this bond on another occasion."

A chill shot down Jeannie's spine, and she shivered. The expression on Carolyn's face seemed almost satanic.

Carolyn's departure was as quick and as unexpected as her arrival had been. She left Jeannie and Loretta in deep silence and thought. Since their friendship had progressed to a stage of complete ease with each other, the need for endless chatter was unnecessary. Jeannie began to clean the kitchen. That boring task suddenly seemed quite simple, and she welcomed the chance to do something with her hands.

Loretta was the one who broke the silence. "I think she's a witch."

Jeannie laughed. "Okay, I'll admit she's weird, but really — a witch?"

"Well, I didn't say she was a bad witch. Maybe she's a good witch. But if you want me to be honest, that title would be overly charitable. You should have seen her at Barry's office today. She reminds me of a snake. You're lucky I rescued your husband from her deadly bite."

"You're overreacting. She just told us some rather earthshaking truths about ourselves, that's all. I'm ready to concede that there might be some validity to her statements."

"Yeah, some validity, maybe. But I'm tired of half-truths and some truths. I'm looking for the whole truth and nothing but." She sighed heavily.

Barry's car pulled into the driveway before Jeannie could rebuff her thoughts.

"Maybe we'd better not mention this to Barry," she said.

But Barry's curiosity instigated the conversation

as soon as he walked in.

"Did Carolyn prove to be a worthy counselor, Loretta?"

"The kind that will send you straight to a shrink," she retorted. She got up to leave. "I see a woman," she said in a monotone. "She is witty, intelligent, and simply gorgeous. And she's got to go feed seven hungry mouths." She laughed. "See you two later."

After she left, Barry turned to Jeannie.

"What was your impression? You usually have a sharp perception of people."

Jeannie thought she saw more in Barry's face than just idle curiosity. "Well, I always feel things about people. I know the instant I meet someone whether I should pursue the friendship or not. But this gal puzzles me. She draws me to her, and at the same time I feel repelled."

"Maybe you should stay away from her."

Jeannie turned to him, wiping her hands on a dish towel. "But I'm so intrigued, Barry."

So am I, he thought to himself.

Loretta drove home slowly, trying to gather her thoughts. She felt embarrassed about the way she had poured out her heart to Jeannie in front of Carolyn. Carolyn was cold and hard and unfeeling, and she knew absolutly nothing about motherhood. Why should she care about Loretta's life?

She stopped the car suddenly, jerking forward as she hit the brake.

"Don!" she cried. "Oh, Don, what's happened? Why do you leave me alone so much? Why do I feel so alone?" She began sobbing heavily, burying her face in her arms.

And she knew. She knew from the moment of her outcry that her husband was never home because she was always on the phone, or buried in some project for the church, or on her way out the door to attend another church function. He was never home because she could never seem to fit him into her busy schedule.

She started the car and drove to the park. She sat for a while, watching the mothers and their children. Her eyes fell on a woman about her age, running from one of her children to the other. She pushed one on a swing, then ran to boost another tiny one up the steps of the slide, then she ran to still another and hugged him as he reached out his arms to her.

She closed her eyes and leaned back in the seat. "Show me how," she whispered. "Somebody show me how."

"If you would direct your heart right, and spread out your hand to Him...

"...you would forget your trouble, as waters that have passed by, you would remember it.

"And your life would be brighter than noonday; darkness would be like the morning."

Job 11:13,16-17 NASB

8
REGROUPING FOR ATTACK

That evening, Loretta walked into her kitchen, took a deep breath, and uttered the most decisive words that she had ever spoken in her life: "Mrs. Miller, I won't be needing you as housekeeper anymore. I've decided to devote my whole life to being a wife and mother."

That had been easy enough, but after the housekeeper left, Loretta analyzed her living room with great disdain. Where should she begin? The children had all deposited their books on the couch and covered them haphazardly with their jackets. Different size shoes of all colors and styles arrayed the floor, along with the toys the smaller children had dumped there.

Jerry's greeting was hearty and warm. "Hi Mom! I'm cooking supper for you. We're having peanut butter and pickle sandwiches." She smiled proudly.

I won't scream, Loretta told herself as she viewed the mess. There was peanut butter everywhere, including on Jerry's mouth and in his hair. *I will remain calm and show motherly appreciation.*

She began wiping up the gooey brown mess, then changed her mind and decided to list everything that needed to be done.

Pick up the den, she told herself, *then bake a cake. T.V. commercials boast of the wonders performed by mothers who bake cakes. Oh, why didn't my mother tell me to fulfill some artistic quest?*

She opened the refrigerator door and took out a carton of eggs, then began to gather together the other ingredients for a cake. She stared forlornly into the bowl as she stirred the flour and sugar together. She was sure Carolyn was wrong about her being bitter and selfish. Did she come across that way? She began to beat the eggs fast and hard. She loved her children! They were priceless jewels. So why had she never felt like she was doing anything right by them? Why this feeling of half-doing everything?

"Mom!" interrupted Paul. "Michael is on the roof."

"What do you mean — on the roof?" Her ears told her that Paul was telling the truth. She heard strange noises above her. She ran outside, looked up at the roof, and gasped. Michael was running, slipping, and sliding gleefully.

"How did you get up there, Michael?" She was trying not to panic.

Michael pointed proudly to the basketball goal.

"Okay honey. Slowly walk over to the pole, and try to come down the way you went up." Should she call the fire department? Did they rescue little boys from rooftops like they rescued kittens from treetops? She looked at her mischievous three-year-old. Out of her seven children, he was probably the primary reason that she had never stayed home. It had been so much easier to let someone else handle him. Oh, wouldn't Carolyn have something profound to say about that!

Michael looked at her innocently, and she suddenly wished she could hold him in her arms and rock him to sleep as she had so many nights when he was tiny...when she was the center of his world. He was just a big baby with a criminal mind, she thought grimly.

After ten minutes of anxious persuasion, the chubby legs hit the ground and flew off to the call of higher adventure.

Loretta watched two-year-old Lucy lick the fudge frosting off of the spoon.

"Would you like to put the pecans on the cake?"

Lucy nodded joyfully and thrust her hand into the plastic bag.

Loretta had had a few moments of peace with her delightful youngest child. She had read the "rabbit book" to her, and they had baked the cake together. The only near obstruction of peace had been Lucy's attempt to pour her glass of Kool-Aid into the cake batter.

"Put your baby in her stroller, Lucy, and we'll take her for a nice walk."

Lucy ran to get her doll, and Loretta watched the brown curls disappear around the corner. She loved all of her children so much. She didn't know why she always talked about them as though they were albatrosses hung around her neck. It had just gotten to be a habit. She tried to remember the last time she had taken a few minutes out to take Lucy for a walk. She suddenly realized that it was possible that she had let Mrs. Miller become a surrogate mother, as well as housekeeper. But that was all over now. Lucy returned, and they walked out hand in hand.

Mother, Lucy, and her baby returned from their walk quite pacified, only to find that the front door was locked. Looking through the window, Loretta could see Michael running impishly through the kitchen toward the living room with the chocolate cake. Kaiser, their St. Bernard, was following Michael, eyeing the cake hungrily and licking his chops.

"Michael Stephen, put that cake down and come open this door immediately!" Michael was oblivious to his mother's pleading voice. "Please don't drop that sticky cake on my floor, Mikey. *Please!*"

Michael soon tired of the game and opened the door. He eyed his hysterical mother with wide-eyed innocence. She grabbed the cake from him seconds before Kaiser reached it.

She greedily swallowed a tranquilizer and half-dozed in an exhausted heap on the couch. After 30 minutes of almost complete silence, she realized that she had not been interrupted by anyone, not even Lucy. She suddenly remembered that Mrs. Miller was gone, and jumped up. Running into the front yard, she spied Paul up in a tree.

"Have you seen your little sister?"

"She went walking with Mikey."

"Oh great! Just terrific! Go check the back yard, honey. I'll look at Alice's house. Maybe they're playing over there."

She found Michael at Alice's house but he claimed that he didn't know where his little sister was. Loretta knocked on every door. She walked up and down streets and alleys calling Lucy, but no one answered her hoarse call. Defeatedly, she decided to call the police before it got dark. Returning home she saw Alice waving to her from her front porch.

"I've been looking for you, Loretta! Lucy was in my house all the time. Michael hid her behind the couch, and told her to be very quiet, because they were playing a game with Mommy."

A game with Mommy, Loretta thought. *They were playing a game with Mommy!* Is this what life was all about?

Whatever happened to the ideal family, the innocence and freshness of family-oriented television shows?

And whatever happened to the ''perfect father image'' that had been so often portrayed in movies?

And whatever happened to the ''model housewife,'' who always stood in the kitchen on a sparkling clean floor, with every hair on her head in place, a clean apron tied around her 23'' waist with a submissive smile on her face?

Loretta looked down at the chocolate frosting on her dress. If Carolyn's dreary philosophy was right, how would she ever handle so many problems alone? Maybe Michael was an enemy from a past life. Maybe he had been placed in her home to seek revenge.

She was going to do it. She was going to have a clean house and well-disciplined children if it killed her. She took Lucy's hand.

''Know where we're going?'' she asked the two-year-old.

Lucy shook her head no.

''We're going to go home and scrub that dirty old house till it shines and then you and I are going to take a bubble bath and fix ourselves all up so we'll look pretty for Daddy when he gets home tonight.''

Fourteen-year-old Joy was waiting in the hall when Loretta got home.

''Mother, what happened to Mrs. Miller? Where's supper?''

''I dismissed her early this afternoon. I wanted to get reacquainted with my family,'' she said lamely.

"You picked a fine time to 'play mother.' I skipped breakfast this morning, and all I had was a doughnut for lunch. I'm starving."

"Joy, I can't hear what you're saying. Ask your sister to please turn that music down."

"You heard what I was saying. You just don't want to listen!" Joy stormed out of the kitchen.

A note was taped to the phone.

Mom, Dad phoned while you were out. He won't be home until the weekend. Betsy.

Incline Thine ear, O Lord, and answer me; for I am afflicted and needy.

Psalm 86:1 NASB

9
GHOST GUESTS

Barry was lazing on the patio in a chaise lounge. Around him, pansies and petunias exposed their tiny heads in the garden. Climbing roses and dark green ferns spread their foliage protectively around the veranda. Splashes of yellow, scarlet, and pink amidst the cool greens created a soft, soothing atmosphere.

Jeannie poured two tall glasses of lemonade while the steaks sizzled heartily on the grill. Resting his book on his chest, Barry peered over his reading glasses at Jeannie. She was wearing a baby-blue dress, his favorite color on her. The dress complemented her hair and eyes. Her flawless complexion, radiating rosy health, pleased him too. He deemed himself fortunate. No problems looms before him now.

Jeannie walked over to him and handed him the glass. She sat down beside him.

"I love it when everything's blooming, don't you?"

"Yeah," he answered. "You've really got a green thumb. It looks beautiful out here."

They sat in silence, watching the sky turn from a deep orange to a bright red as the sun began to set.

"Penny for your thoughts," he said.

"Make it a dollar and I'll think about it," she said, laughing. "Oh, I was just thinking about Carolyn. After she talked to Loretta the other day, she intimated that my life and hers were also linked together in some way. Would you object if I consulted her a few more times? She's shown me a lot about myself.''

The topic of conversation dampened Barry's mood. His brow furrowed. He had exercised this habit so frequently that his forehead was permanently wrinkled. Jeannie playfully ran her finger over the crease on his brow. Her gesture dispelled the foreboding premonition that had arisen with the mention of Carolyn's name. Jeannie assumed that his silence meant that he approved.

Their solitude was interrupted by the sound of loud music.

Angrily, Jeannie said, ''Barry, this is the fourth time today I've tuned that radio off. The children aren't in the house to turn it on now, and earlier they were in school.''

''That isn't the only strange occurrence around here,'' Barry said. ''Did you know that three times this week the light has suddenly gone on in our bedroom? Once it happened in the middle of the night, and I turned it off twice last night.''

''I know. At first I thought our house was just settling. I even thought for a while that the children were playing tricks on me, but now I'm sure they don't have anything to do with it.'' Jeannie looked frightened. ''This scares me. Judy's books are full of stories about ghosts.''

''Don't be absurd, Jeannie.''

''I'm not being absurd! There are logical explanations for their existence. A dead relative may be trying to get our attention.''

''Why?''

''To help us maybe.''

"I'm afraid I don't consider having to turn lights off in the middle of the night helpful, Jeannie." He reached over for his napkin, threw it over his head, and yelled "Boo!"

Jeannie jumped, startled, then stood up. "Laugh and make fun of me, if you must. But sometimes I feel a presence, one or more, near me. If I could look hard enough I could see who it is. I could reach out and touch that presence." She frowned and stared at the ground.

Jeannie's thoughts alarmed Barry. She had always been so sensible and down-to-earth. She had become so withdrawn since their move to St. Matthew's Church. She was introverted and he wished she would become involved with new people. She had always painted beautiful rural scenes, but her interest in painting seemed to be waning.

He decided to call Loretta. Maybe she could get Jeannie busy in some activity that would distract all this morbid thinking.

The phone rang and Jeannie rushed to answer it. The voice on the other end was deep and resonant. "Care for another visit into the unknown?" asked Judy.

The uncanny timing of the call unnerved Jeannie for a moment.

"Barry thinks I have too many visitors from the unknown already. I don't think he's in the mood for any cute parlor tricks."

"That's too bad. I wasn't thinking of anything amateurish though. I was talking about taking another journey into your past. Carolyn's here and we thought we might drop by if you're not busy."

"Barry has a meeting at eight. Why don't you come then? I'll have coffee ready."

"A dry, white wine would be more appropriate for the occasion. See you at eight."

Jeannie hung up the phone as Barry walked in.

"Secret admirer?" he asked, smiling.

"No," she said thoughtfully, missing his humor. "Just Judy. She and Carolyn are coming over tonight." She walked back outside, not seeing the frown on Barry's face.

"You said something strange on the phone, something about visitors from the unknown." Judy watched the champagne bubbles dance rhythmically in her glass.

"Yeah, we've had some strange things happening at our house lately. Buzzers, lights, the radio, the stereo, the television — they all pick inopportune times to come on. But that's the least of our problems. I haven't told Barry this but the children and I have seen outlined forms of people! I thought I was hallucinating at first until the kids mentioned it too."

Jeannie watched their faces, knowing they wouldn't be shocked or even surprised. Carolyn looked indifferent and Judy just looked interested. Jeannie knew that they had psychic experiences all the time. She didn't know why she wasn't more alarmed herself at what she and the children had seen, or thought they had seen. Things like this just didn't happen every day!

"How long have these things been happening?" Judy was asking.

"For a few weeks, maybe even two months, I'm not sure. At first I just thought we were having bad dreams, since it happened usually at night." Jeannie glanced at Carolyn, who was smiling slightly. She wished Carolyn would say something, instead of sitting there with that all-knowing look on her face. She made Jeannie feel like a child.

"Anyway," Jeannie told Judy, "a few nights ago, Charles said he saw an oriental man walking behind me." She started to laugh at the absurdity of the statement, but Carolyn and Judy looked serious. "He told me about it very matter-of-factly and began to describe the man's attire in detail. He said that he wore a funny little hat, had a funny long pigtail, and that he wore a multicolored long robe. And Mary had an experience that really frightened her. The sound of footsteps awakened her, and she said she saw a white-haired lady standing at the foot of her bed. The old lady carried a candle. On different occasions the children have described their vision of a large, bearded man. They usually hear his footsteps before they actually see him. They say that he's rough and wears boots."

Jeannie paused to sip her drink. "I've heard voices several times. I've always considered myself to be a rational human being. What's happening to us? Your books are interesting, Judy, but I think I'd rather read about these things second-hand."

Carolyn had been listening intently for a change. Her eyes would become large and then narrow to cat eyes. They even changed colors, Jeannie had decided, but they remained predominantly yellow and green.

"You have psychic powers, Jeannie," she said suddenly. "And obviously your children do too. I've known instinctively that you and I were predestined to work together.''

''There you go again, tantalizing me with those isolated statements again,'' Jeannie said. ''Okay, I'd like a full explanation now.'' She was surprised to hear her own voice exhibiting authority to Carolyn. The usual faraway look in Carolyn's eyes caused a tinge of anger to spark in Jeannie. Sometimes Carolyn's aloofness was maddening. Who did she think she was? She was available only if her mood swayed her.

Jeannie knew she might as well not expect this woman to open up and be friendly; she was as unmovable and as cold as an iceberg. Yet people were drawn to her, and Jeannie knew she was another victim. The realization of Carolyn's magnetism made Jeannie even madder.

Carolyn still hadn't spoken. Her posture stiffly erect and her eyes looking steadily and directly at the bookshelf, she walked over and removed the ''R'' volume of the encyclopedia. Maintaining the same air of indifference she turned the pages until she reached a picture of a Roman house.

Jeannie looked at the house blankly, then looked up into Carolyn's eyes. Was it supposed to mean something? Carolyn suddenly looked to Jeannie as if she were surrounded by a cloudy mist. Jeannie closed her eyes for a minute, deciding that she had had too much wine. She opened them again and stared at Carolyn, who was gazing back at her. The mist was still there and she watched with disbelief as the haze seemed to leave Carolyn and envelop her! For some reason she found herself thinking about the era of the Roman Empire, and the architecture and lifeless people on the page of the book came alive. Jeannie suddenly felt that she knew them, how they looked, how they pursued life, how they loved and how they hated.

She could see herself in the picture, in some life long forgotten. She watched herself, a young girl of wholesome beauty, seated in a luxurious chair. Her light brown hair and large doe eyes justified her simple, green gown. The beautifully but simply furnished house gleamed with tile and marble. Fresco paintings hung with huge magnificence on the walls. Seated by the pool, she was awaiting a guest in the atrium.

Her young man approached her. Rain began to fall softly through an opening in the roof into the pool. She reached out her arms to greet her lover, but they never embraced. Something was wrong. Someone else was present. Someone else was always present, casting a dark shadow on her bright, childlike world.

She turned her head slightly to view the other person, a beautiful, young girl with feline qualities, with changeable eyes, eyes with shades of yellow and green — irrepressible, haunting eyes that widened and narrowed.

Jeannie looked up from the page and stared in fear at Carolyn, at the ram with the woman's breasts hanging around Carolyn's neck. She knew now why she felt intrigue and terrifying repulsion whenever she encountered Carolyn. They had loved the same man many lifetimes ago.

Trembling violently from the impressions she had just witnessed, *Jeannie acknowledged that the man was unmistakably Barry!*

Noonday boasted of light, warmth and healing, but Jeannie sat listlessly in her darkened den. Every curtain had been drawn tightly. She flinched slightly and pushed a wayward curl back as the phone rang again and again.

Had she allowed friends to enter her home, they would not have recognized her. Her long, worn, granny robe lent a strange protection to her tired body, but her appearance gained nothing from it. She slumped in a corner of the couch, unaware of the rapid deterioration of her house. Three cups stained with coffee and tea, a saucer holding half a stale sandwich, and a cold bowl of soup disarrayed the coffee table.

She watched the various entities come and go brazenly through the darkened passageway of her life. The old lady, carrying a candle, tried to light her way. Hearing footsteps behind her, she often turned to see the oriental man with the long pigtail. The frequent presence of the white-haired man caused a slight smile to initiate on her lips.

Only the bearded man upset her. She found his roughness irritating and his presence unnerving.

At first she had been frightened by what she was seeing. But time had changed all that. They were a part of her now, a part of the darkness that was her life.

No, she did not fear them, but every time the doorbell or the phone rang, she was filled with an irrepressible fear. She feared the face of a friend or a loved one. She could not pinpoint when this strange, foreboding fear had begun. She only knew that her life energy was slowly slipping away, bit by bit.

She pulled her feet up and lay down on the couch, covering her head with her arms.

"Blessed are those who hunger and thirst for righteousness, for they shall be satisfied."

Matthew 5:6 NASB

10
BATTLE OF SPIRITS

The worry lines on Barry's face created a fixed geometric pattern. After the phone rang six times, he answered it reluctantly. He didn't want to speak to anyone.

Betty Small's bland voice, interrupted by occasional sobs of self-pity, echoed endlessly in his ear. The dull tone of her voice gave him an opportunity to escape into his own private thoughts.

He was concerned about, even afraid for Jeannie. His once energetic, bright-as-a-penny, slightly sarcastic Jeannie. Even the sarcastic quips were gone. Jeannie simply did not care. Something (he had an idea what) had slipped into the very core of her personality and robbed it of life.

Loretta had attempted to reach her, but Loretta was having her own problems. She too had experienced deep depressions. She had relinquished all her busy work in the church and was spending every moment in motherly endeavors. He smiled slightly, recalling his last encounter with Loretta. He had gone to visit her, afraid she might be sick since he hadn't heard from her. Her house looked like a tornado had struck. She came huffing and puffing to the door wearing a gray sweatsuit, and said she had just pedaled a mile on her new exercise bicycle. She seemed to be able to ignore the mess. He missed her work at the church, yet he was glad to see her attacking her problems at home for a change. At least she was trying....

A pleading note in Betty's voice pulled his attention back to the phone conversation again.

"John doesn't pay any attention to me," she was saying. "He tunes me out completely. He hangs on to every word Pat says though," she added bitterly.

Every encounter group session had harvested more disastrous results, thought Barry. Pat's and John's flirtation had gotten steadily more intense with each meeting. One hideous night the group had decided to spend that meeting paying each other compliments, in an effort to bring out a kind of positive reinforcement. Tension mounted as Pat listed John's virtues, and Betty had ended up crying.

Betty announced somewhat cheerfully at the next meeting that she and John had spent the next night "communicating," but Barry had spent many sessions with Betty, patiently distributing Kleenexes to her, and he knew that Pat and John were now having an affair.

Even Judy's tough exterior had been broken by her husband's preoccupation with younger women. And Janet and Tom, who had been innocently drawn into the group, were experiencing marital problems.

Where had he failed? The caliber of entertainment had been excellent, and certainly inspirational. Psychics, astrologers, and writers, all eminent and prestigious, had been main speakers. The attendance had grown rapidly and steadily.

Barry had been particularly pleased the evening that the astrologer addressed the group. The astrologer had fun noticing character traits of people, and the people in the group were amazed as he told each of them about their individual sun signs.

Transcendental meditation had been introduced into the group too, and several people had raved of almost instant peace and help. But the peace was short-lived, and they began to experience personality problems.

Jeannie had missed it all, and Barry silently grieved about her withdrawal. He couldn't understand her reluctance to see Carolyn, whose enthusiastic personality and eye-catching beauty had captivated the group over and over again. He couldn't help but \compare Carolyn's vibrance with Jeannie's lack of any vitality whatsoever. Jeannie barely even spoke to him anymore. He was lonely. He needed her more than ever now.

Jeannie was once like Carolyn, full of plans and ideas and energy....

"How flattering that you are thinking of me."

Carolyn's sudden appearance unnerved him as always. Betty was saying something about calling him back another time, but he barely heard her. He hung up the phone.

Carolyn walked over to his desk. He stared at the vision before him. She was strikingly beautiful in black. *Black emphasizes her dark eyes,* he thought. *Only I thought that her eyes were green.*

"Grandmother always had fun dressing me as a child. My chameleonic eyes change colors constantly."

He smiled uneasily. "You are a very spooky woman. Do you always read people's thoughts?"

She sat down. "Why should it bother you? Actually, it has its advantages. For example, I know where a beautiful hand-designed jacket is that happens to be just your size. You should take advantage of clothes. You're a very handsome man, you know.'' She cocked her head to one side. ''You know you're handsome, don't you?''

Barry ignored her question, but she persisted in carrying on the coquettish conversation.

''I told you that you needed my counsel and advice, Barry. I'm the only one who can help Jeannie. The psychiatrist treating her has failed miserably. You haven't been able to reach her with love. Loretta hasn't been able to reach her with friendship. She's in a complete state of withdrawal.''

''How do you know all this? Has she talked to you?''

''Jeannie hasn't talked to anyone.'' Barry observed Carolyn's all-knowing expression, and he detected a hint of boredom in her voice.

He couldn't understand why he was drawn to her physically. He didn't even like her. He had never liked cold, aloof women who acted as though they were untouchable. He loved Jeannie. He always had. But his Jeannie did not exist anymore. In her place was a person he had never known. She did not respond to him or to the children. The laughter that had once prevailed in their house had been silenced. Sometimes he heard her talking softly at night, but when he questioned her, she would look at him sadly and withdraw once more into her shell. He didn't know how to restore her. He thought that maybe this strange woman sitting in front of him might hold the key that would unlock the door deep in Jeannie's psyche. He needed advice desperately.

''Why don't you ride with me to my place in the country? I can always concentrate better there. I know you want to rush home to Jeannie, but she's safe in a world you cannot enter. She will not respond if you go home. It will only be a repeat of other past nights, all running into a stream of sameness. You can help her more by going with me. I can give you insight into her problem.''

She moves like a cat, he mused. He studied Carolyn as she glided across the room carrying two drinks, the ice clinking rhythmically as she walked. Her eyes became all-consuming as she neared, her presence having both a dizzying and unreal effect. He devoured the drink, which left a taste of both bitterness and sweetness in his mouth. He had never tasted anything like it and he would ask her what it was later.

The open window allowed the scent of sweet olive to fill the room with its pleasing fragrance. Carolyn removed the gold clamp that smoothed her hair back, releasing an abundance of luxurious black hair. She reached for a magnolia blossom from a vase on an antique table by the couch and fastened it in her hair. The white magnolia contrasted seductively with her black hair. She climbed into his lap in a fashion both predatory and cuddly. He recoiled for an instant, then buried his face in her hair, drinking in the sweetness of the magnolia. The stairs creaked as he carried her to her bedroom. The magnolia blossom lay on the floor, abandoned.

Jeannie glanced at her calendar. Her head ached as she tried to relate to the activities that had slipped by in the past few weeks. She had tried to come out of this depression, to carry on life as usual with the children, Barry, the church, the group, and friends, but she couldn't seem to relate their lives to hers.

She knew something was wrong with Barry. A terrible blackness enveloped her when she thought about him: an uncontrollable fear. She wasn't sure what it was that she feared. She couldn't remember. Perhaps it was the unknown. An incredible, pounding headache pulsated at the back of her head with every small noise. She would not try to think. It no longer mattered anyway. She no longer wished to be a part of the world. Her own situation was more than she could cope with.

She had slept late, and managed to walk from the bed to the couch. She automatically turned the television on. A trim, smartly dressed lady was speaking. She wore a blue dress accented by a sharp red jacket and red accessories. Her makeup was applied immaculately. Her voice had a soothing and hypnotic effect.

She spoke about meditation, and emphasized that a person could capture the heart of God by concentrating on the beauty of a rose or any other object in nature. She emphasized too that the mind should be completely blank to receive joy and peace. This meditation, she assured her listeners, would rid the mind of all inner turmoil. She claimed that she was the minister of a church which believed in the Christ, the theory of reincarnation, transcendental meditation, astrology, and all psychic phenomena.

She then invited all interested people to attend her church.

Jeannie sat up suddenly as a phone number and address flashed across the screen. She quickly dialed the number, and a friendly voice answered. Jeannie said something about needing peace and knowledge and the voice promised perfect healing by meditation on the "Christ" by concentrating on streams of water and mountain scenery.

The voice stressed the importance of the Christ and His place in the creativity of life and in the creativity of the soul. The picturesque, peaceful scenes of streams and mountains became momentarily alive in Jeannie's mind, and an aching desire to meet the lady minister with the soothing voice stirred in her.

Jeannie waited to meet Rev. Susan Matthews in a room unlike any church parlor she had ever seen. The parlor was a rented ballroom in a hotel. The chairs were lined up in long rows, and long tables, laden with books, surrounded the chairs. Jeannie recognized many of them as being the same books introduced to her by Judy. Huge pictures of Jesus hung on the walls. Decoupaged scriptures and biblical scenes held prominent positions in the room.

Why did she feel uncomfortable and afraid? Everything in the room certainly looked innocent enough.

She checked her watch impatiently. She wished the lady reverend would be prompt for their appointment. This was the first time she had ventured from her house in weeks. She was pale and weak. She wanted to run from the room, back to the safety of home.

People began slowly filtering into the room. The topic of the lecture for this Monday night was to be "Reincarnation — Where Do You Fit In?" Jeannie wondered why she had responded to the lady minister. She had not responded to anyone else, but a flicker of recognition had briefly illuminated her mind when she had talked to the woman on the phone. She knew she had been looking for truth for a long time; she knew she would instinctively recognize truth when she found it. So she found herself here, in a meeting, surrounded by strangers, looking feebly for an answer.

A large lady walked in and sat behind one of the tables. She smiled invitingly at Jeannie, indicating with a gesture that many books were available. A slight chill went up Jeannie's spine. The lady was not Carolyn, and yet there was something of Carolyn in her. Carolyn. That name, that face. That presence that seemed to manifest itself in other people. Jeannie couldn't remember why she feared her.

Every head turned as Rev. Matthews walked briskly into the room. The small woman was wearing a red blouse, a gray skirt and vest and very high heels. The color of her eyes was hidden by her false eyelashes, and Jeannie decided that even her most distinct features were hidden by heavy makeup. Her manner exuded the same magnetism that Jeannie had witnessed on television, but she suddenly wished that she had not come. She did not like her.

The reverend approached her and held out her hand.

"Hello, I'm Reverend Matthews." Her voice was somehow condescending. Jeannie felt like she was being talked down to.

"I'm Jeannie Holstedt," she said weakly.

"Oh yes. I've heard of your husband. His intelligence and progressive views are to be commended. I just attended an Edgar Cayce convention. I was amazed to see all of the different denominations represented there. Very inspiring. I met outstanding laymen from Baptist, Methodist, Presbyterian, and other churches. They did not particularly want their views brought out in the open. But your husband has taken an open stand in his views. And now his wife has paid me an unexpected call." She looked at her watch. "It's almost time to begin. Why don't we talk after the meeting?"

She walked off before Jeannie had a chance to answer. All eyes focused on Jeannie as she tried to find an inconspicuous place to sit. She was feeling increasingly uneasy. Dare she get up and walk out? Watching Susan Matthews' methodical and overly self-assured mannerisms reaffirmed her dislike for the woman. Jeannie had sought a compassionate friend, and instead had found a cold, unfeeling machine.

Cheerful music emerged from the piano as five girls appeared and sang songs about rivers and sunshine. They wore neat blouses and short plaid skirts which revealed the tanness of their legs.

The reverend began to lecture and familiar details clicked in Jeannie's mind. She had heard most of this before. She talked about children, and explained that most small children are psychic and can remember details of their former lives. Many times, she said, children have recognized family friends from past lives. She also explained why some children are more advanced intellectually, attributing this phenomenon to the fact that those child geniuses are simply "older souls." She talked about the importance of each person's finding something out about his former life so as to grow steadily more aware of himself.

Many hands applauded her lecture and a long

line formed to shake hands and to commend her. A young man, awkward and obviously very unsure of himself, walked up to the reverend. "Everything you said really hit home, ma'am. I've always wondered about that sensation of having been somewhere before or the feeling that I already know someone that I've never seen before."

Jeannie watched the reverend's face as she smiled coldly at the boy. She was looking at him as though he were ignorant and something only to be tolerated.

Jeannie slipped through the crowd unnoticed. She had to get outside where she could breathe.

The starry night did not comfort her or still her fears. She had taken a cab earlier, but she decided that a brisk walk might be therapeutic and would give her time to think. She vaguely wondered about the people who lived in the white-trimmed look-alike houses. It was so quiet! Were any of them lying in bed as she did every night, wondering if they could face another day?

She saw a man in the foggy distance leaning against the corner street light. He looked familiar, but she was alien to this neighborhood. Even the battered brown jacket on his thin frame looked familiar. She admonished herself, thinking that Susan Matthews' lecture had taken its toll.

The old man turned and walked slowly down the street, and Jeannie was relieved to see that they were headed in the same direction. She wasn't sure why she was compelled to follow closely behind him, but every sure step he took made her feel more certain that he was aware that he was guiding her. But where?

The moon cast a soft light on a small chapel in front of them, magnifying its steeple and lonely cross.

The old man climbed the steps of the chapel slowly, then turned and looked at Jeannie with a face that could only be described as loving and radiant. Jeannie told herself that it was entirely too soon for another church encounter, yet she ascended the steps and followed him through the door.

She detected something quite unique in the countenances of the men who greeted her. Their faces radiated a beautiful light. Fascinated, she allowed them to lead her to a seat. There was a bustle of excitement and enthusiasm all around her, and she contented herself by surveying the room of smiling faces.

She could no longer see the face of the old man in the crowd, but she observed the faces around her that undoubtedly experienced real communion, even friendship, with God. A small, gray-haired lady put her arm around Jeannie; her whole being offered her love.

After she had watched the people around her for a few minutes, Jeannie switched her attention to the church itself. On both sides of her were handmade scrolls on the walls, each bearing a different scripture. Each sheet of parchment was a different soft, pastel color, and she could tell that they had been done by children.

She read them one at a time. The one nearest her said, ''Prepare Ye The Way of the Lord,'' and next to the words was a trumpet with musical notes rising from its opening. Another scroll was soft yellow, and written on it in a darker yellow was ''Ye Are the Salt of the Earth!'' and beside it was painted a salt shaker, spilling its salt over a globe. Jeannie smiled, thinking of her own little Charles' vivid imagination. Another scroll said, ''Our Father which art in heaven, Hallowed be thy name.'' She smiled again, remembering the day Mary had asked her why God's name was ''hollow'' and if that had anything to do with ''Halloween.''

Another scroll was made of soft pink parchment and was beautifully bordered with tiny, hand-painted roses. Its message read: ''Blessed are they which do hunger and thirst after righteousness: for they shall be filled.'' She swallowed hard and looked toward the front of the church. The view made her catch her breath. It was beautiful! There were wildflowers everywhere, and she could tell that they had been gathered from the countryside outside the town. There were daffodils and marigolds, daisies and baby's breath. They had been placed in containers of all shapes and sizes — some were even in tin cans. And above them all, a beautiful scroll hung from the ceiling. It was made of fine, white parchment and on it, in bold letters, was written, ''Come unto me, all ye that labour and are heavy laden, and I will give you rest.''

A youthful minister appeared at the front of the church, and he beamed like everyone else in the room. Jeannie was now engaged in a private game of measuring the obvious light that surrounded the people. The minister looked exuberant, excited. His eyes shone, and he looked from one face to another as he spoke.

''Jesus Christ is here tonight,'' he said, smiling broadly. ''He is Lord. The day is soon coming that every knee shall bow and every tongue confess that Jesus Christ is Lord. He is walking through the aisles and touching each of your lives just as He walked through the crowds 2,000 years ago. He is the same yesterday, today, and forever.''

Spontaneously, people began to praise Him in song:

He was wounded for our transgressions.
He was bruised for our iniquities.
Surely He bore our sorrow,
And by His stripes we are healed.

No one directed the people in song or in praise. Jeannie could no longer see the young minister, yet the service flowed in perfect order and harmony. People began to give testimonies.

The gray-haired lady declared that she had been healed of arthritis.

''I was healed of worry, anxiety, and fear,'' stated a young housewife. ''He delivered me of all my fears.''

"The doctor confirms healing of my cancer," said a man.

Many praises were lifted to the Lord as many more testimonies were given.

Songs sung in a language unfamiliar to Jeannie filled the chapel. *They must be highly intelligent, too,* she thought. *They even know other languages.*

She turned to see a vision of purity as a young woman sang a love song to God in a language Jeannie couldn't understand. Her eyes were closed and her arms were raised, as if she were reaching out for Him. After she finished, another lady began singing the same song in English:

How I love you, My children.
My children, please come.
Come to your Father,
Come through My Son,
Come for atonement at My throne.
Cast away all of your sorrow.
Rid your heart of all pain.
There's a brand new tomorrow,
A new start, a new land.

A hush fell over the room as the young pastor began his simple sermon, telling of God's great plan of reconciliation. He said that the Holy Spirit had been sent to convict the world of only one sin, unbelief in Jesus. Belief in Jesus, believing that He was raised from the dead and confessing Him as Savior made us "new creatures." The young pastor also proclaimed that Jesus was raised in glory and honor, and that He was standing at the right hand of the Father interceding for us. The minister emphasized "good news" and love.

The service ended with more singing and praise. Jeannie wanted to stay, and no one else seemed to be in a particular hurry to leave. After some time, with much laughter and caresses, the group departed, leaving Jeannie seated quietly in the candlelit church.

The flickering light of the candles revealed the old man in the brown jacket kneeling at the altar.

Little children, let us not love with word or with tongue, but in deed and truth.

1 John 3:18 NASB

11
MIND CONTROL

The rain beat forcefully against the large picture window in Jeannie's den. Its cleansing action gave renewal and life to the large and small-leafed plants — the caladiums, petunias, pansies, and geraniums that decked her flower bed with bright colors.

As the rain subsided, she watched through the window as small droplets rolled lazily off the banana, schefflera, and rubber plants. The light mood of the preceding night was distant and removed from her thoughts. She wished that water from heaven would fall on her thirsty soul and give her the cleansing that her garden was experiencing. But the rain only aroused irritation and anger in her.

She had returned home very late the night before, but she had still preceded Barry. He was coming home late every night now.

The events of the previous night had made Barry's personality change seem all the more real to her. His short temper and frequent sudden outbursts of anger were becoming almost uncontrollable.

He had become extremely fastidious about his clothes. He demanded perfection in matching colors, and he was particularly interested in the feel of the materials. Every few weeks he would dispose of his old clothes and replenish his wardrobe with new materials and ostentatious fashions. He claimed that his body became "desynthesized" to certain materials and that each new wardrobe signified a higher spiritual level. His flamboyance was sometimes replaced by depression. He then refused to communicate with anyone.

Jeannie remembered her amusement the first time Barry had begun to have this sudden interest in clothes, in textures and colors. (Had it been two months already?) He would stand in front of the mirror and scrutinize himself, pulling his stomach in and throwing his shoulders back. She had figured he was just beginning to feel middle-aged and that this new interest in his looks was merely an attempt to hold on to his youthful good looks. She had begun to compliment him often, although she sometimes felt that he had gone somewhat overboard in his choice of clothes. (Once, he had walked in wearing brown pants, a bright orange print shirt, and a painfully clashing orange tie. She had had to bite her lip to keep from laughing.) But lately his obsession with clothes had begun to alarm her. It was becoming all-consuming. He was wearing his clothes as though his looks and overall image were the single most important thing for which he had to live.

She stood up and walked into the bathroom. She looked at herself in the mirror for a long time. Did she look old — was that why Barry was drifting away from her? Had she turned into such a monster in the last few weeks that he had to stay away from home as much as possible to avoid her?

She brushed her hair with an angry gesture and tied it back with an orange ribbon that matched her housedress. She stared at her image again. She had lost weight and looked tired, that was certain.

She wondered briefly if she would ever again hear Barry say, "You look and act like my old girl."

That thought irritated her even further. She wondered which Barry she would face today.

Barry's booming voice answered her silent thoughts as he descended on the morning with great wrath.

"Why didn't you iron my shirt?" he demanded, waving it in front of her. "You know the image I present is highly important!"

Before she could retort bitterly, he charged into the children's rooms, demanding their immediate presence at the breakfast table. Charles and Mary, sleepy-eyed and bewildered, stared at their father. Their lives had been confused lately. Their mother had refused to play imaginary games or to read to them for months, and now their once calm father was irrationally angry. They hurried out of bed and ran to the kitchen.

The pancakes stacked golden brown awaited the company of butter and blueberries. The coffee steamed in Barry's favorite mug. Jeannie watched him angrily stirring cream into his coffee, and for a moment she felt sad and truly sorry for him.

Could she have been too involved in her own problems to consider Barry's plight? If only she could remember how this nightmare had begun! But all of her reflections gave no feasible answers.

Barry knew Jeannie was staring at him. His memory was as hazy and confused as Jeannie's. Carolyn now held the key that motivated his thoughts and actions with amazing precision. He couldn't remember the moment when she had begun to control his life. He only knew that he was a puppet and that the strings were manipulated by an exotic and dangerous woman.

Magnolia blossoms, strange-tasting wine, and ever-changing eyes that demanded and seduced had changed a mild, compassionate man into a boisterous, noisy minister who seemed to cause nothing but disunity and disturbance in his flock.

As he stared into his cup of coffee, he recalled the day that Carolyn had appeared brazenly at church. She had walked slowly down the aisle after the other members had been seated, and sat conspicuously in the front row. Her gray dress was no eye catcher, but her presence was manifested in a spectacular way. There were low whispers and a general turning of heads as she sat down directly in front of the pulpit where he stood.

Barry had looked steadily into Carolyn's eyes that morning and was enveloped by waves of recollection. He had voiced disapproval, cynicism, and skepticism when their relationship had first begun. He had wanted to resist this beautiful woman, yet he was bound to her by forces he couldn't fathom, enslaved by her beauty and suggestiveness. The country air and the old house had soothed his troubled mind, and Carolyn had fulfilled his sexual needs. His resistance had easily broken down and he had succumbed to her every suggestion.

He thought back to the day Carolyn had taught him to meditate. It had been warm outside, and they were sitting in her living room drinking wine. The hum of an old-fashioned overhead fan was soothing and he was feeling lightheaded and pleasant.

"Transcendental meditation is what Maharishi Maheh Yogi taught some famous singers of the sixties," Carolyn had told him. She was dressed in a colorful caftan and lay sleekly on the couch. "Many astronauts and congressmen meditate twice a day, as well as some noted football stars, an actress, singers, and one of the president's experts whom I could name."

He interrupted her. "I remember hearing of a famous actress' pilgrimage to the Maharishi in 1969. I thought the whole thing was weird. I associate this whole process with eastern religions."

"You're not getting narrow-minded, are you, Reverend?" Her voice was teasing. "I don't see how something that improves one's self-esteem can be so misunderstood. It's not allied with a far-out religious cult. Many knowledgeable, respectable people are meditators. The Pentagon has a meditation room. Wall Street brokers and corporate executives practice T.M. and a grant from the National Institute of Mental Health is used to train high school students and teachers to meditate. It has been reported that drug addicts in federal prisons are being helped through it, and that T.M. has the blessing of the army as a potential cure for alcoholism and addiction in the ranks. Medical tests show that it lowers blood pressure, alleviates asthma and helps smokers...."

"Okay! Okay!" Barry said, laughing. "You've convinced me. You've certainly done your homework, fair lady. Okay, exactly how do you meditate? Where do you start?"

"The secret is in the sound your teacher gives you. That sound, called the *mantra,* is a word but it doesn't mean anything. It's just there to help you to forget everything else around you. You close your eyes and repeat your *mantra* to yourself, over and over, and gradually you drift off into a meditative state. *Mantra* is a Sanskrit term — it really has nothing to do with hypnosis, psychiatry, or philosophy. The transcendental state is an ancient technique originated by the Vedas. This state is different from the other three states of consciousness: sleeping, waking, and dreaming. It's merely an activity to relieve stress.

"I usually meditate twenty minutes at a time, twice a day. It slows down the heartbeat, decreases oxygen intake, and makes the blood circulate vigorously."

Barry sank into the deep club chair and eyed a painting that hung over Carolyn's fireplace. She followed his gaze.

"That's a painting of the late Guru Dev, the philosophy teacher, who in 1941 began the present worldwide revival of T.M. by teaching it to any worthy person who asked to learn it." She looked at Barry again. "You must have a teacher, Barry, and I am qualified. I will tell you your *mantra* and you must keep it a secret."

"I suddenly have visions of dancing gurus," Barry said, laughing. "But I'm curious. How will you select my *mantra* and why am I supposed to keep it a secret?"

"*Mantras* have never been recorded on paper, but have been passed along orally from teacher to teacher through the centuries. Vedic scholars developed the technique in the fourteenth century B.C. I must base your *mantra* on your birthdate, your educational background, your job and leisure activities, and on all of your intellectual and psychiatric experiences. To be successfull you must guard the secrecy of your *mantra* and learn the proper technique for its use.''

A despondent and faraway look passed over Barry's face.

''You're thinking about Jeannie, aren't you?''

''A man can't help but think about his wife after thirteen years of marriage. I've never denied my love for her. You know that.''

''I can understand your feelings. But that's exactly the point of this whole conversation. You need to be relieved of all that guilt, and the stress that results from it.'' She leaned forward and whispered a word in Barry's ear. ''Now close your eyes and think of that word over and over. A thought may come to you that is stressful or upsetting, but continue to repeat your *mantra* and the stress will disappear. It takes concentration, but if the *mantra* seems to be slipping away, just let it go. Don't hang on to it. Now, just sit back and relax.''

Barry leaned back, closed his eyes, and concentrated on the sound of his *mantra*. The sound was pleasant, though meaningless. He thought of Jeannie. He saw the golden tanness of her arms and legs. He saw her habit of pushing her honey-colored hair out of her face. He heard her rippling laughter and associated it with the pleasant sound of their favorite brook.

Then he saw the present Jeannie — tired, listless, and unresponsive. His breathing became shallow. His world slipped away. He began to float into an existence of perfect peace and harmony. He felt clean and clear inside. He decided that he would be stronger and more compassionate from then on.

He had immediately experienced a surge of energy, and from then on he had not felt tense or tired as he counseled with people. The endless piles of papers on his desk did not harass him, and the constant interruptions did not bother him. Whenever he began to worry about Jeannie's condition, he would retreat to his room. The children and outside noises coming through the window were often distracting, but he would concentrate on his word until everything else was blocked out. At times his head would fall almost to his chest and his neck would hurt. He performed rituals with fruit and flowers, chanting all the time in Sanskrit. This was his offering of thanks to Guru Dev for sharing his knowledge with him. He practiced for twenty minute periods twice a day. He had felt compelled once to substitute nonsense syllables for his word, and that had resulted in a severe headache, queasiness, and irritability.

For a while he was vitally alive and sharp, and conducted his services with magnetism and vibrance. But personality changes were subtly taking place.

He snapped back to the present.

Yes, Carolyn's brazen appearance in church unnerved him. He had difficulty concentrating on his prepared sermon. Other voices and thoughts intervened, but he thought that surely the voices had always been there directing him. They were an integral part of his personality.

"Why are you always so predictable?" the voices asked, taunting him. "Look at your new image, your impressive clothes. Everyone is sitting on the edge of his seat in anticipation. Your beautiful mistress has made her entrance. They want to see a show! Your sermons should be as unpredictable as your new personality has become. You are a unique individual with original thoughts and philosophies.''

His voice resounded through the building. ''Let the one among you who has not sinned cast the first stone!'' he shouted.

He paused and looked down the rows of startled faces. He searched for the right words, the perfect words that would shock these people and make them see that they were being led by a man of intelligence, originality, and ambition. A man who could show them how to be better, more enlightened individuals. A man who had found himself and attained peace through self-awareness.

He suddenly found himself revealing special secrets about different individuals in the congregation, betraying privileged information. He indicated that one member of the congregation was hooked on prescription medicine and was supplying her daughter with needed pills daily. One prominent deacon, he said, had a problem with alcohol. A certain lady in the congregation was guilt-ridden because she did not wait a respectable period of time to resume life's activities again after her husband's death.

Several people stood up and left, and some looked as though they would like to leave. But many sat with their eyes glued to the magnetic figure at the front of the church, waiting for his next words.

Barry ended his sermon shouting ''Hypocrites! Hypocrites!'' Robed in black and wearing a shiny cross, he exited as dramatically as his mistress had entered.

Therefore if any man is in Christ, he is a new creature;
the old things passed away; behold, new things have come.
2 Corinthians 5:17 NASB

12
CREATURE WITH POWER

Jeannie sat in the car staring at the dashboard as she waited for the car to warm up. She could hear the children next door shouting and laughing with their friends. She wondered how she could have closed the door and locked them out of her life for the past three months.

Things were still bad for her. She still stayed home most of the time and preferred not to see anyone. But she was also beginning to yearn to get back to her old self again.

She knew it would be a slow process, "climbing" out of her reclusion back into the world around her, but she desperately needed to get away from that house, and she longed for companionship.

Her meek reentry into life was bringing her face to face with some harsh realities. She was hurt and puzzled by Barry's behavior. It had started as an ego trip, but now it had turned into a battle of sorts, a battle that he was fighting against her and against himself. He was energetic one moment, and the next moment she would find him sitting in his room or in his favorite rocking chair on the patio in an almost catatonic state. Neither personality state resembled the Barry she had known for almost fourteen years.

Her tears of anger and bitterness did not reach him. And in those moments when she would try to reason with him he would literally run from her, and stay away from home for hours.

She knew that somehow their experimentation with the unknown paralleled their problem, but she couldn't imagine why, or how. Barry's goals were high-minded; they always had been. So how could evil manifest itself in good? How could perversity come from someone who had always tried to help everyone around him? It didn't make sense.

She desperately wanted to talk to someone, but she had severed almost all ties of friendship within the last months. Loretta had tried persistently to reach her for a long time. Maybe she would welcome a visit.

She backed out of the driveway, waved to the kids, and drove to Loretta's.

The outside of Loretta's house looked different. The yard wasn't cluttered with bikes, skates, and toys for a change. Its manicured appearance indicated that Loretta had either gotten a green thumb or had hired professionals to arrange the boxwoods, azaleas, and ligustrums with such precision.

Loretta responded immediately to Jeannie's knock , but Jeannie didn't recognize her at first.

"Hello, is Loretta...?" Laughing, Jeannie realized her mistake and exclaimed, "My gosh, you've lost so much weight, and your hair's different, I love it!"

"I'll gladly accept that as an apology," said the slender lady with frosted hair, smiling. "Come on in, Jeannie. I've missed you."

If Loretta's physical appearance had amazed her, the house amazed her even more. There was still evidence that nine people lived there, but it had a warm, welcoming, orderly look. She had control of her home! Jeannie studied her serene face, and decided that Loretta had an inner peace that her physical body could not contain.

They sat down in the breakfast nook where the dewy freshness of morning befriended them. Loretta served coffee and blueberry muffins hot out of the oven.

"I'm not going to mince words, Loretta. I really need a friend, and I need advice. I know you've heard rumors about Barry and Carolyn. But now that I'm here I'm more intrigued by the change in you. What in the world has happened in your life?"

Loretta did not reply for a moment. She gathered her thoughts silently and carefully. She had a precious story to relate, and she didn't want to destroy its freshness with impulsive chatter.

"Jeannie, when you last saw me my life was in complete chaos. You know that. And the more I strived to fit myself into the roles of wife and mother, the more chaotic it became." She paused for a moment, then continued.

"I was visiting with a neighbor one morning. It was a friendship that I'd never cultivated because she always seemed to have complete control of her home and her kids and her presence made me feel more insecure than ever. Anyway, I commented that morning that I'd always both admired and envied her ability to cope with her family life so easily." Loretta laughed. "She's one of those women who always looks terrific but you never see her with curlers in her hair."

Jeannie smiled.

"Well, she smiled as though she had a secret and she confessed that her life hadn't always been that way. She said that Jesus Christ had become her special friend when she received the baptism of the Holy Spirit. She didn't elaborate on that point or define exactly what the baptism was. She dropped the subject and continued to sit there looking disgustingly happy. I was admittedly quite irritated by her apparent simplicity, and I decided that I didn't want to be around her. But her happy face loomed before me continually.

"I called her a few weeks later and asked to know more about her personal relationship with Christ. Whatever it was that she had, I wanted some too! She invited me to a attend a charismatic meeting with her that evening, a meeting where people practiced what she called the gifts of the Holy Spirit. Well, that meeting proved to be the most revolutionary experience of my life." Loretta grinned happily.

"The meeting was in someone's home and when I walked in the door I immediately noticed that the room was full of shining, happy faces. As Marcia introduced me to her friends, they each embraced me. I witnessed genuine love and concern in every embrace. It wasn't like they were doing it as a routine gesture; it was as if there was a bond of love flowing from one person to another. Soon they joined hands and sang simple songs that seemed to spring from their...well, their inner beings.

"'Halleluia...Halleluia...Halleluia' was sung over and over again and they sang with raised hands,
He is Lord, He is Lord,
He has risen from the dead and He is Lord.
Every knee shall bow and every tongue confess
That Jesus Christ is Lord.
"I wondered why they raised their hands while

they sang, but I read recently the scripture in First Timothy 2:8 that says, 'I will therefore that men pray every where, lifting up holy hands, without wrath and doubting.'

"The people began singing faster, and they began to clap their hands joyfully and a few of them began to dance. At that particular point, I began looking for a way to escape." Loretta laughed. "I've always thought that such frivolity in church is sinful, and was certainly not biblical. But Jeannie, I now know that David danced before the Lord, and he was considered to be a man after God's own heart! Psalm 47:1 for instance, declares, 'O Clap your hands, all ye people; shout unto God with the voice of triumph,' and Psalm 98:8 says, 'Let the floods clap their hands: let the hills be joyful together.' I wonder who's been hiding the news that Christians are supposed to be happy!"

Jeannie was staring at her hands; she looked profoundly sad.

"You want some more coffee?" Loretta asked her.

Jeannie nodded.

Loretta refilled their cups and continued.

"The prayer time began just as spontaneously as the singing. The prayers were simple:

"'I thank You, Lord, for fixing things. You fixed my schedule, my child's hurt leg, and even my broken-down car. I thank You that You fix things.'

"'Thank You, Father, for sending Your Son. We do not deserve such love.'

"'Praise Your holy name. We love Your Son. We love the Holy Spirit. We worship the three in one.'

"'I praise You for the washing and cleansing of

the Word. Thank You for revealing Your nature to us in Your Word. We look forward to Your soon return, Jesus. Even all of nature groans in travail for Your coming.'

"'Jesus, You are worthy of praise. Worthy is the Lamb that was slain. We praise the Father that You are not still on the cross. You are resurrected and are standing at the right side of God the Father Almighty making intercession for us as we pray.'

"It became obvious to me that they were really *talking* to God and that a beautiful communion had developed between them. The meeting continued with testimonies of healings, stories of how God had supplied every need spiritually and materially. A hush fell over the room and a man began to speak in a language unfamiliar to me. Although I couldn't understand what he was saying, I was impressed by the authority with which he spoke. After he finished there was a moment or two of silence, and then someone else began to interpret in English what had been said. It went something like this:

I am the Good Shepherd. If you will come to Me, I will give you living water to drink. You will never again be thirsty, but you will be beautifully supplied. My well never runs dry. You did not choose Me, but I chose you before the world was formed and I have ordained you that you might go and bring forth fruit. The harvest truly is plenteous but the laborers are few. The fields are white for harvest. The time nears that I will harvest My saints. Do not try to lift the sickle yourselves. It is too heavy. You must come to Me, the vine, so that I might supply you with life. How I yearn for you to return to Me. How I love you. Even nature groans in earnest expectation of My return. Behold! I stand at the door knocking. My return is near.

"The following silence was comforting. I wouldn't

have been surprised if a voice had said, 'Take off your shoes, Loretta. You're standing on holy ground!'

"About that time I was frantically wondering who the leader of this group was. The meeting was conducted in a beautiful order of worship yet no one person seemed to direct it. Then different people began to quote scripture. A burden lightened in me as the scriptures flowed from one thought to another."

Loretta stood up. "Let's go into the living room. I wrote down some of the scripture references so I could go back and read them later."

Jeannie followed her reluctantly. She had had plenty of scripture lessons in her life and this was not what she needed now. Not today of all days. She needed to talk. But Loretta looked so excited and Jeannie hated to hurt her feelings.

Loretta walked over to the bookcase and pulled out a Bible, from which she withdrew a slip of paper.

"All I had to write it all down on was the water bill," she said, laughing. She motioned for Jeannie to sit on the couch, then sat beside her and opened the Bible.

"Okay, this first one really 'blew my mind,' as the kids say. It's Psalm 95:1-7." She began to read slowly:

O Come, let us sing unto the Lord: let us make a joyful noise to the rock of our salvation. Let us come before his presence with thanksgiving, and make a joyful noise unto him with psalms. For the Lord is a great God, and a great King above all gods. In his hand are the deep places of the earth: the strength of the hills is his also. The sea is his, and he made it: and his hands formed the dry land. O come, let us worship and bow down: let us kneel before the Lord our maker. For he is our God; and we are the people of his pasture, and the sheep of his hand.''

She turned to Luke 12. "I want to read you Luke 12:22-28. It's a scripture that really meant a lot to me. It talks about how unnecessary worrying and anxiety are:

Therefore I say unto you, Take no thought for your life, what ye shall eat; neither for the body, what ye shall put on. The life is more than meat, and the body is more than raiment. Consider the ravens: for they neither sow nor reap; which neither have storehouse nor barn; and God feedeth them: how much more are ye better than the fowls? And which of you with taking thought can add to his stature one cubit? If ye then be not able to do that thing which is least, why take ye thought for the rest? Consider the lilies how they grow: they toil not, they spin not; and yet I say unto you, that Solomon in all his glory was not arrayed like one of these. If then God so clothe the grass, which is to day in the field, and to morrow is cast into the oven; how much more will he clothe you, O ye of little faith?''

Jeannie closed her eyes and leaned back. The scriptures were soothing, and they offered comfort and bright promises. But life wasn't made of sugar and spice and bright tomorrows. Loretta wasn't aware of...couldn't see the ugliness in Jeannie's life. She was swept up in a fairy tale world of pretty words and heavenly thoughts. She didn't know what it was like to wake up every day and face a cold, unloving husband who couldn't wait to get out of the house. She could talk about peace all day long, but Jeannie hadn't known peace in a long time and she couldn't even remember what it was like. Words that had been written 2,000 years ago couldn't apply to her now, not in the sorrow that was her life.

"God promises us that the peace which passes

all understanding will keep our hearts and minds in Jesus," Loretta said. "He says that He has swept away our transgressions! Our sins are like clouds that return to Him — He's redeemed us, Jeannie. He compares His name to a strong tower, and He says the righteous man runs into this tower and is safe. This means there's nothing to fear; there's nothing too big for God to take care of for us. 'God is our refuge and strength, a very present help in trouble,' and His Word, the Bible, is a lamp to our feet and a light to show us where to walk.

"And all we have to do is ask. When we ask Jesus into our hearts in a simple prayer, He comes in. And He lives there, and brings us the kind of joy we can't find around us in our families, our material things, our jobs. I know you've experienced some of that joy, Jeannie, but you've also let the people and things around you draw you right down to where Satan wants you.

"I know more about what's going on in your life than you think I do. I know what grief you're going through right now and I'm sure your whole life and your problems must seem irreparable. But God says to *love* your enemies and to *pray* for the people who persecute you. 'And my God will supply all your need according to his riches in glory by Christ Jesus.' It doesn't have to be a power play when you're letting *Jesus* do the loving through you!"

Jeannie caught her breath. "And my God will supply all your need..." How many times had she quoted that scripture as a child? How simple and promising those words had seemed to her when she would sit in church as a little girl and fold her tiny hands together in prayer.

The church of her childhood had been much like St. Matthew's. The sun had shone cheerfully through its windows and that church, too, had sat on a hill. The congregation would sing loudly, hymn after hymn, and the minister... She closed her eyes again. She didn't want to think about Barry now.

' "All things are possible to him that believeth' " Loretta read. "When Jesus said that, He wasn't talking to just a small group of people around Him. He was giving a promise to all of mankind — you and me, our husbands, our children and their children. Jesus said in Mark 16:18, '...they shall lay hands on the sick, and they shall recover.' "

Loretta paused for a moment to allow Jeannie to think on that verse. Then she went on. "A man who sought healing for deafness sat down on a chair in the middle of the room and several people placed their hands on him, along with a man who led in prayer.

"The man testified that he could now hear clearly! He was so excited. Then a lady limped forward, and I watched her shortened leg grow even with the right one while everyone prayed.

"Then someone asked if anyone would like to receive the baptism of the Holy Spirit. I looked around the room, wondering if anyone was going to respond, and suddenly this man looked right at me and started talking to me as though he knew the silent questions I was asking.

" 'Loretta,' he said to me, 'I am reading from John 16:7-13 in *The Living Bible*. Jesus is talking to His disciples before He is crucified:

"It is best for you that I go away, for if I don't, the Comforter won't come. If I do, he will — for I will send him to you.

"And when he has come he will convince the world of its sin, and of the availability of God's goodness, and of deliverance from judgment. The world's sin is unbelief in me; there is righteousness available because I go to the Father and you shall see me no more; there is deliverance from judgment because the prince of this world has already been judged.

"Oh, there is so much more I want to tell you, but you can't understand it now. When the Holy Spirit, who is truth, comes, he shall guide you into all truth, for he will not be presenting his own ideas, but will be passing on to you what he has heard. He will tell you about the future.' "

''Then the man showed me how Jesus' promise of the baptism with the Holy Spirit was fulfilled. He showed me Acts 2:17,18 where Peter stood up to preach on the day of Pentecost:

'''In the last days,' God said, ' I will pour out my Holy Spirit upon all mankind, and your sons and your daughters shall prophesy, and your young men shall see visions, and your old men shall dream dreams. Yes, the Holy Spirit shall come upon all my servants, men and women alike, and they shall prophesy...'''

''Peter declared that if men would turn from sin, return to God, and be baptized in the name of Jesus Christ for the forgiveness of their sins, then they would receive the gift of the Holy Spirit.

''When Simon the magician saw that people received the baptism of the Holy Spirit when the apostles laid hands on people, he offered them money for the gift. Peter rebuked him, because it is a free gift from God.

''Jeannie, I had been baptized as a child, but I had never lived a victorious life. I yearned to know Jesus and to have the power to testify about His death and resurrection. Several people knelt down by my chair and prayed softly. I heard the words, 'Jesus Christ is the baptizer.' I thought that surely everyone could see the beautiful light that filled the room. I was overwhelmed by a love so gentle and pure, an unconditional love.

"In an instant, I knew that I had met a friend who could fill the empty gap in my life, fill it with security, give assurance of His ever-present love, and give me a deep joy like I'd never known before. No wonder Paul was changed so radically when he saw the vision of Christ on the road to Damascus! I was convicted of sin, but it was instantly covered with His love.

"*Instantly covered with His love,*" Loretta repeated. Then she shook her head slowly and smiled. "I knew then that my searching had ended and that the Spirit of life had breathed on me and made me a new creation.

"Then, in the rapture of that moment, I began to speak in a glorious new language. Have you ever heard anyone speak in tongues, Jeannie?"

Jeannie nodded yes. That was what she had heard the night at the little chapel.

"With each new word that came from my mouth, I was enveloped and edified in love and joy. It was contagious. Many of the people around me began to laugh joyfully, and that's when I understood why they were such a happy group.

"When I got home, I found that I had a new companion within me. I wanted to speak in my new language continually. The Holy Spirit is the divine psychiatrist. As I spoke in my prayer language He revealed deep hurts and scars to me. I didn't consciously remember some of them. As He revealed each hurt, He touched the hurt gently, healed it, and removed it. I see this not as a panacea, but as a beginning. I share a portion of God's immeasurable love and mercy as I commune with Him. When Jesus walked on earth in the flesh, He was limited by time and space. But through the Holy Spirit, He is available to all who will receive the gift freely. That's a promise!

"Oh I still have a lot of problems, but there's a difference now: I'm a problem solver! When I speak in my new language, I can feel resentments, anger, and frustrations leave. Paul mentions speaking 'with the tongues of men and of angels.' I think God desires for His people to speak to Him in a Spirit language frequently.

"In 1 Corinthians 14:2, Paul says that 'he that speaketh in an unknown tongue speaketh not unto men, but unto God: for no man understandeth him; howbeit in the spirit he speaketh mysteries.' When we speak in tongues, we're speaking directly to God in a language He gave us for that purpose!

"As I told you, Jeannie, I've known Jesus as my Savior since I was a child. A lot of us have. And we spend our lives going around doing things we think we ought to do, like giving a few dollars here and there to charity, or visiting a sick friend, or not cheating on our income tax, things like that. And when the chips are down, when there isn't enough money to pay the rent or when a friend dies, we turn to God and pray a quick, three-minute prayer and then forget about Him until the next crisis.

"But that's not much of a relationship! That's just an on-again, off-again type of relationship. If I only saw you once every month or two, and we tried to get to know each other in just a few minutes each time, we wouldn't be very close. We would practically remain strangers, in fact.

"And that's just the way it is with God and man. When Jesus comes into our hearts, when we ask Him in as our Lord and Savior, we're going to miss out on so much if we don't take advantage of our friendship with Him. I don't invite guests into my house and then ignore them for days or weeks at a time. Yet that's what I've been doing all my life with God.

"What I'm getting at is that I've discovered Jesus as my *Lord*, as well as my Savior. I didn't have to give up anything, or pray extra hard, or try to be a better person. I just stepped out in faith and told God that I was botching things up — that my husband and I weren't getting along, that my house was a wreck most of the time, that sometimes I wanted to sell my kids! I handed the whole thing over to Him, picked up a dust cloth, and things have been falling into place ever since, or rather He's showing me how to put them in place. But Jeannie, this skinnier Loretta you see with the clean house is no miracle compared to what's happened inside me. I've got a joy like you wouldn't believe! I'm *enjoying* being alive today, not wishing today would be over so I could get on to tomorrow.

"The Bible says that we haven't received because we haven't asked. God is my spiritual Father now, and you can bet that I'm going to take advantage of it. I'm going to run to Him for everything — every bruised knee, every budget that won't balance, every parking place I can't find downtown. He says to 'pray without ceasing,' and that's just what I'm doing. I want Him as my Lord and there's nothing I'd like better than to depend on Him for everything from now on. Through the baptism with the Holy Spirit, I've found new life.''

Loretta had talked for over an hour and Jeannie hadn't interrupted her. She was awed by Loretta's story, but she was also a bit irritated. She had come here looking for a pat answer to her problems and had received a scripture lesson instead.

She stood up, found her purse, and fumbled through it for her keys. She made an excuse to leave and politely thanked Loretta for the coffee and her time. Loretta hugged her and told her that she would see her soon.

She looked back at the house as she drove out of the driveway. Loretta was waving and smiling from the front porch.

Jeannie waited until she had pulled away from the house before she burst into bitter tears.

"Do not turn to mediums or spiritists; do not seek them out to be defiled by them. I am the Lord your God."
Leviticus 19:31 NASB

13

IN THE CLUTCHES OF MEDIUMS

Barry and Carolyn sat across from each other in her living room.

Each meeting with Carolyn had tightened the reins on Barry's life. He was now convinced that he had a special mission to fulfill, that he must feed his flock with his new-found discoveries. He must relentlessly fulfill this mission at whatever cost. The voices that he had begun to hear during his meditations guided him daily now, often through Carolyn's counsel. They told him that he was an individual, a man in his own right, and a man who must lead others in their quest for truth.

Today he wore a cool, blue silk shirt with puffed sleeves, brown slacks, and boots. Through her trances, Carolyn had advised him in finding the right outfits in his size. His clothes became more elaborate as he passed from one level to another.

He looked thoughtfully at Carolyn. She was sitting erect in a cane chair, her legs crossed underneath her. He thought of what she had done for him. He was no longer living a hypocritical lie. He was leading people to find themselves and to accept themselves as unique individuals. He felt proud of himself. He knew he and Carolyn drew people to themselves magnetically.

A small group of people usually followed them.

Some were merely curious, but others were genuinely interested in his project. He worked hard to appeal to all outcasts in society, especially those who had been discriminated against. Those people were totally accepted no matter how far they had deviated from the normal. People with sex hangups would be especially welcomed. He and Carolyn would create a utopian environment where they could develop the creativity within each individual to its highest level.

"I have an eminent question to propose," he said. "What is our assignment for today?"

Carolyn's face changed expressions, assuming a pained look as she listened for instructions from the voices. Her voice sounded deeper than usual as she began to speak. "It is urgent that you organize your people and find a serene place to live together in harmony. You must first rid your life of all unnecessary material possessions, before you can give your project full attention and servitude."

Barry's eyes whisked swiftly around the large room. The antique grandfather clock in the corner manifested its presence by chiming five times. He looked at the unusual assortment of vases, the old wood tables, the barren oak floor covered here and there by faded rugs, and the big windows that exposed moss-laden trees. This was the setting in which he had spent many afternoons and evenings, and he felt comfortable here.

"I can't think of a more serene retreat than this one," he said quietly.

Carolyn nodded approvingly. "Thinking this would be your choice I took the liberty of inviting several followers over for the evening."

She walked over to the dusty closet and began to

pull canvases off the shelf.

"These are some of my latest paintings. We'll need a substantial income to get our project going. I studied the astrological signs of the people coming tonight, then I painted pictures of each person. Can you see how I placed each person in a setting which best emphasizes their personality traits?"

She held up a painting of a charging bull. The dainty figure holding the cape was Pat Miller.

Barry withheld comment about the painting. "I thought we were going to avoid material encumbrances."

"I interpret that to mean material possessions linked with your marriage, and some of the unnecessary possessions I have kept," she said. "We must sever all past ties." She pointed to the canvases. "These are products of our new lives."

The sunset, illuminating a pink-and-yellow-cast across the room, reminded them that their guests would soon arrive. A cloud of dust polluted the shades of pink with the arrival of Clyde Conan's black Dodge.

Clyde wore a long black robe, reminiscent of his days of priesthood. Through Carolyn's influence and his search for truth, he had joined the group and was now one of its strongest leaders. Since Clyde had joined them, Carolyn had noticed that Barry was allowing him to take over the lead in many of the group meetings. The room was soon filled with an odd assortment of people — two homosexuals, several women who flagrantly expounded their lesbian ideas, an astrologer, a phychic, and a young teenaged boy who had run away from home. Occasionally Judy would attend a meeting.

They were all assembled and discussing future plans when their conversation was interrupted by a timid knock. The door opened slowly and the moonlight exposed the frail figure of Pat Miller. She was shivering fiercely from the damp night air and she looked frightened.

Wrapped in Carolyn's green wool robe and seated by the crackling fire, Pat related her story.

"I know that you're the only ones who can help me. I grew very close in this past year to a lady named Gladys. I spent a lot of time with her the last six months of her life. She had terminal cancer. Even though she was in much pain, she always had a cheerful attitude, and I really grew to love her. Well, it became difficult for her to do little things for herself, so I spent evenings styling her hair and fixing supper for her and her husband Tad.

"I was relieved when I heard about her death, because I knew that she had finally been released from all that pain. I remember looking at her lying in that coffin, free at last from her burdens, and I realized that it was not she, but merely a shell of her former self. But I was not released from that friendship." Pat stopped and looked at the faces around her. She wasn't sure if she could put into words what had happened to her. She sipped her tea, then spilled it from the cup as she set it back on the saucer. She wished she could stop shivering.

"The night after the funeral, I tossed and turned, unable to sleep. I became aware of a presence in the room with me. I sat up straight in bed and as my eyes began to adjust to the darkness, I saw her. I saw Gladys! She looked much younger than I remembered her and she wore a pale blue dress that emphasized the reddish highlights of her hair." Pat stared into the fire and the others could see that she was back in her bedroom reliving the vision of Gladys.

"Her lips moved but I couldn't understand what she was trying to tell me. The fact that she was there didn't frighten me. What frightened me was that she was so frantically trying to relay a message to me, and I couldn't understand. I can still see her standing there, her lips moving, her arms flailing wildly, her eyes flashing desperation, defeat, and perhaps even anger. Then she faded away. She's appeared to me three times in the last two months."

Pat paused to pull the woolen bathrobe tighter around her. The faces closed around her in anticipation.

"Last night I had the most realistic dream about Gladys," she continued. "She said she had an urgent message to tell her husband and that I was the only one receptive enough to help her. She kept saying 'Help me. Please tell Tad. Help me talk to Tad.' I awoke abruptly from the dream before I could understand the rest of her message." Pat looked around her, searching their faces for some sign of their reactions to her story. "So you can see my plight, can't you? I must communicate with her."

Clyde was the first to respond to her unusual story, He stood up suddenly.

"I was compelled to come here rather than fulfill another engagement tonight," he said, walking over to Pat and taking her cold hand in his. "Nothing in this world in ever accidental, Pat. I've conducted many seances successfully, and I can help you contact your friend."

Pat hesitated a moment, then sighed deeply.

"I just want to be sure that I'm doing the right thing," she said, so softly that they could barely hear her.

"Uh-huh. We understand that. I'll read scriptures to you in a minute to show you how right you were by coming here." He began to pace up and down the room, looking up at the high ceilings. "This house is perfect!" he exclaimed. "I love this old place." He walked to the fireplace and rested one arm on the mantle. "I like the feel of it — the tall ceilings and large windows cast the perfect stage for a seance. Spirits love roomy locations. I believe the dining room will be the best place in the house for it. And I can see Carolyn thinks so too."

He laughed and pointed to the dining room table which was visible from where they sat. Carolyn was already busily making preparations for their guests. The curtains were drawn, and she was lighting a kerosene lamp that gave the room a dimly lit effect.

"You've probably surmised from my attire that I'm a priest, an excommunicated priest, I should say," Clyde told Pat. "But don't let that concern you. Most people aren't enlightened about the spirit world and don't understand about its link with God. It is all one, all unity. These spirits do much to communicate with us and to give us information about our present lives as well as life in the hereafter. Some, for example, have advised people about astute business moves to make.

"People just won't open their minds enough to let the spirits help them." Clyde frowned and stared into the fire for a moment. The room was silent. He looked down at Pat and her eyes searched his face for some hint as to why he looked so irritated. He suddenly looked sheepishly around him, realizing that they were all staring at him, waiting for him to continue.

He sat down on the couch. "Often while praying for someone's healing," he said quietly, "I have seen the spirit of an old man or woman standing by the person I was praying for. I believe that these spirits are instrumental in their healing. While watching a four-year-old child prodigy play the piano, I saw a spirit controlling his hands. That's certainly one theory for the phenomenon of child geniuses, as far as I can see. Since I believe this activity to be linked with the reality of God, I would like to quote several scriptures to you proving the validity of reincarnation and the spirit world.

"Exodus 21:23-25 states: 'And if any mischief follow, then thou shalt give life for life, eye for eye, tooth for tooth, hand for hand, foot for foot, burning for burning, wound for wound, stripe for stripe.' So if you killed someone in your last life, then you are a target for death in your present lifetime.

"Jesus was asked in Mark 9 why the scribes said that Elias must first come, and Jesus said that Elias had already come and restored all things. They realized that He was talking about John the Baptist, the reincarnation of Elias.

"My favorite quotation of Jesus is this one in John 3:7-8: 'Marvel not that I said unto thee, Ye must be born again. The wind bloweth where it listeth, and thou hearest the sound thereof, but canst not tell whence it cometh, and whither it goeth; so is everyone that is born of the Spirit.' Do you see how the Bible supports the theory of reincarnation, Pat?"

She nodded uncertainly.

"You must be born time and time again until you are perfected," Clyde said, standing up. "I'm going to light a candle for Mary the mother of Jesus." He leaned forward, took a candle from the coffee table, and lit it. He walked through the house, the strange procession of people following him. He placed the candle in the center of the redwood dining table, and everyone sat around it.

"The power of concentration is very crucial at this moment," Clyde said. "Let's hold hands to increase the power of suggestion."

He sat at the head of the table with Pat on one side and Carolyn on the other. Barry sat at the other end of the table. A few people began chanting softly while the others sat very erect, staring ahead. The chanting continued for about fifteen minutes, and then a strong silence permeated the room.

Clyde began to speak. "I feel the presence of my Indian guide. His name is White Feather."

Pat, deciding that she had made a terrible mistake, began to watch Clyde fearfully. His body began to shake convulsively. Then he slumped over onto the table. In her fear, Pat instinctively thought he had died. After a few minutes, he sat up again. The deep bass voice that came from his mouth was not his.

"I am White Feather. I bring you salutations. I have desired a meeting with you. There is quite a gathering here from the other side. There is someone who would like to speak to you."

"We are desiring special communication with Gladys Day. Is she in your company?"

"She is. If you will focus your spiritual eyes, you

will see her standing between you and Pat."

Pat spontaneously jerked away from Clyde, and to her it seemed like her hand brushed against a soft, invisible form. She gave a cry of surprise and was aware of a hand resting on her shoulder.

Pat was consumed with fear but she wanted desperately to communicate with Gladys. Her voice was weak, and she couldn't keep her hands from trembling violently.

"Gladys, is that you?" she asked. "Please, I haven't been able to sleep for nights. What are you trying to tell me?"

In her mind she saw the soft, green chiffon dress first, then she envisioned Gladys plainly and was convinced that it was she.

White Feather began to speak once more through Clyde. "Gladys wants to assure Tad of her safety and happiness. He has been very grieved. She watches him almost constantly. She watched him read a book the other night. The book was *Passions of the Mind*, and he stopped reading on page 186. She only mentions this to prove that she was there. He put the book on the nightstand when he finished reading, and she placed it properly on the bookshelf. She also tidies up the house for him. He always forgets to put his slippers in the closet.

"She asks Tad not to grieve for her. She is safe and happy. Many friends and loved ones were awaiting her arrival on the other side. They have done much to help her adjust and to comfort her. She says that she has been given an assignment. Several children have been put in her care.

"Uncle Steve sends his best to Tad, and advises him not to pursue any new business ventures for several months. The man that Tad has been dealing with will soon have a change of heart."

The room was silent for a few minutes. Carolyn stood up and turned on the light, and the members of the group began to talk about the messages from the Indian.

Pat stared at the candle. She felt she had seen Gladys and was convinced of the validity of the experience, yet she felt fear still, as though something was still missing.

Barry walked over to her and invited her to stay at the big house for a few days or weeks. She agreed. She was divorced now and her affair with John had ended, and she decided that living in the old house might help her straighten out her life again. She needed to have people around her.

The group talked a while longer, then retired to various rooms in the old house.

Pat lay in bed and stared at the ceiling most of the night.

And after you have suffered for a little while, the God of all grace, who called you to His eternal glory in Christ, will Himself perfect, confirm, strengthen, and establish you.

1 Peter 5:10 NASB

14

THE KILLER THIEF

Jeannie drove home slowly. The song Loretta had sung earlier kept running through her mind: *"To God be the glory for the things He has done! With his blood He has saved me..."*

She looked around and realized that she was almost to her own street, though she couldn't remember the drive from Loretta's. She stopped at a stop sign and watched as a man and woman embraced on the sidewalk next to the car. They parted, then turned around and waved to each other.

"God is our refuge and strength," Jeannie said out loud. Where had she heard that scripture before? Barry. It had always been one of his favorites. Psalm 46. "God is our refuge and strength," she said again. "A very present help in trouble."

She turned the corner, and saw cars and a group of people gathered around her house. The people seemed excited and confused. Maybe the commotion was at the house next door. No, it was definitely her house. People were putting things into their cars and leaving. She parked the car and ran to the front porch, searching for Barry or the children.

"Are you going to give it *all* away, preacher?" a robust, ruddy-complexioned man was asking Barry. He had a notebook in his hand and a camera around his neck.

Barry answered affirmatively by smiling and raising both hands in a light gesture.

Jeannie bumped into a lady who was carrying one of her antique chairs. She couldn't believe her eyes.

"That's one of my favorite chairs!" she cried. "What's going on around here?"

"*Was* your favorite chair, sister. It's mine now."

Two sturdy men carried the heavy French provincial couch toward a waiting truck.

Jeannie saw the curtain move and glimpsed Carolyn's black hair in the window. What on earth was *she* doing in her house? Hadn't she affected their lives enough?

She walked briskly over to Barry. "What's the meaning of this?" she asked, her eyes flashing with anger.

"They directed us to give away all material possessions," he answered. He avoided her eyes.

"Who directed you? I don't know what you're talking about, Barry."

"The voices," he said, still not looking directly at her. "The voices directed us to give it all away."

"What do you mean, voices?" She felt hot tears of anger spring to her eyes. He was crazy! Or was he possessed of an evil spirit?

Her hands suddenly clenched into tight fists and she ran toward the front door, toward Carolyn, then changed her mind and walked slowly back to Barry. What could she say to make him realize that he was doing exactly what Carolyn had wanted all along — breaking up his home and shutting out his family from his life? Couldn't he see the deception? Didn't he know that she was a treacherous woman who only wanted to possess everyone around her so that she could hang them around her neck like some trophy

148

medal?

"Barry," she said slowly, "I've been very tolerant through all of this, partly because my attitude toward your ministerial position has been so bad. I'm also much to blame for your involvement with Carolyn. It was my interest in the occult that started this... this quest into the unknown. But now I suspect that you are very sick."

His face transformed into a taut expression. His eyes narrowed and his voice was accusing.

"She told me you wouldn't understand," he said. "You've never understood or supported me. Now I have an opportunity to serve a great cause, a cause that could easily culminate in world peace. At the very least it could produce inner peace in individuals who are alone and searching."

He grabbed her by both shoulders, stared at her intently, and pushed her aside fiercely.

World peace. Inner peace. She could only compare the spirit of meekness in Loretta with Barry's hostility.

There was a crowd outside now; most of them were curiosity-seekers. Barry's name had been in the newspapers — one reporter had called him "the minister with a not-so-regular message." Jeannie had to escape the crowd that was gawking at her and Barry.

Tearfully, she entered the barren house that had once been the home she had so carefully and lovingly decorated. But it was not completely empty. Carolyn stood in the middle of the room defiantly. Jeannie thought she looked like a misguided, rebellious child.

"Admit you've lost, Jeannie. You've lost again," Carolyn said coldly. "How many lifetimes? How many times will it take you to learn?"

Jeannie looked calmly and steadily into the large green eyes. "It is appointed to man once to die and after that the judgment." (She wondered where she had picked up that bit of information.) "No, I haven't lost, Carolyn. I haven't lost my mind, my husband or my children. The search has been long, but I believe that this is the moment of truth. I actually have a deep pity for you, Carolyn. You may never find contentment. I'm not sure yet how I'll fight you. There are some things I don't understand myself. But one thing is certain. I will fight with the power of Jesus Christ." Jeannie marveled once more at her own words.

Carolyn's reaction was unexpected. Jeannie watched her exhibit disbelief and then fear.

Carolyn turned suddenly and fled from the house into the crowd outside. Suddenly a young man ran forward and yelled at her as she ran to the car.

"Witch! Witch! Preacher's witch! Adulteress! Homebreaker!"

Jeannie's sobs could not drown out the accusations that were being hurled at Carolyn outside, nor could she drown out the violent protests of Barry. Wasn't the age of stoning past?

She slumped to the floor and buried her face in her arms. The outside turmoil was beginning to subside as Barry went out and said something to Carolyn, then returned. He stared at Jeannie blankly, then walked into the bedroom and closed the door behind him.

Now I have the other Barry to contend with, Jeannie thought. *The quiet, sullen, defeated Barry. The one I would like to mother and comfort like a small child.*

Charles and Mary ran into the room where she sat, and threw their arms around their mother. They were wide-eyed and frightened.

"Children, I want you to walk to Loretta's house. Tell her that I would appreciate it if you could stay there for the night. She'll understand. Tell her I'll call her later."

They turned and started to leave, then paused and turned back to look at her. She ran over and put her arms around them.

"It's okay, sweethearts. Mommy just needs to talk to Daddy." She hugged them hard. "Go on now. Charles, hold Mary's hand when you cross the street."

They walked out just as the phone rang.

The voice on the other end of the line was low and unrecognizable. "Just thought you ought to know...."

Jeannie hung up the phone numbly. She had received dozens of calls the last few weeks. Some were threatening, some sympathetic, and others were obscene. Mostly she found them to be torturous, gossipy, and unnecessary.

She rummaged through her purse for an aspirin, then realized she had left her bottle of aspirin in the car. She opened the front door to go out and almost collided with the bishop. She gasped and stepped back. He was easily recognizable. He was a big man with a red, bland face. They had met him a year ago in his business-like office. Barry had been the bishop's bright-eyed boy wonder then.

Jeannie motioned for him to come in. As he walked in, Barry walked out of the bedroom and stared at them. He looked beaten.

And suddenly the bishop was bellowing angrily at Barry in merciless tones. He berated Barry for what he had become, for what he had done to his family, his church, and the community. He called him a disgrace to his profession.

Barry stood there, listless, unable to refute the accusations. He left Jeannie alone to defend him as he walked into a world of complete withdrawal — out of the role of prominent young leader and into the role of defrocked minister.

"Whoever drinks of the water that I shall give him shall never thirst; but the water that I shall give him shall become in him a well of water springing up to eternal life."

John 4:14 NASB

15
SEDUCING PSYCHIC POWERS

Jeannie walked down the same shaded street, past the same white-framed houses, and up the steps of the same old church. But it was not the same day. It was a new day, and she felt joy and expectancy in every step. She wondered briefly about the old man who had led her there the first time.

The church was empty, yet the feeling of sacred belonging remained. She wasn't sure what she expected to find. She sat in the back, surveying each pew and remembering some of the people who had sat there that night with upraised hands and radiant faces. The empty cross stood simple and alone on the pulpit.

The sun cast a slight hue through the stained glass windows on the portrait of Christ. It was her favorite picture of Him. He was standing with His arms outstretched. He wore a loose, white robe and His brown hair hung wavy and soft, almost to His shoulders. His smile was gentle and comforting.

Then she looked up toward heaven as though looking into the eyes of the real living Jesus. She didn't know how long she basked in the quiet presence of Christ, five minutes or an hour — it didn't matter. Time stood still while she drank in the living water of the one who said, "I am Alpha and Omega, the beginning and the ending." She knelt humbly in His presence and said simply, "I'm tired of my way. Show me Your way."

Soft music and singing began to fill the air and she gazed ahead startled, thinking that she was about to witness a heavenly choir. The music was coming from the vestry, and she stood up and followed the words, "Jesus, Jesus, Jesus! There's just something about that name!" to a half-opened door. The meeting was apparently ending, and she watched several people leave until only an elderly man was left standing there, reading a sheet of paper.

He saw her and walked toward her. "How can I help you, my dear?"

"You don't know me," she said slowly. "I don't belong to your congregation. But I'm sure you've heard of my husband, Barry Holstedt. His name has been in the news quite frequently lately. Unfortunately that's why I need to talk to someone."

"I'm Brother Raymond. I was just getting ready to have lunch. Won't you join me? You can tell me your story while we eat, where we won't be disturbed."

She nodded, and the elderly man led her to his office. He sat down slowly in his worn leather chair and motioned for her to sit in a big stuffed chair across from him. The housekeeper entered and set the table for two.

"My name is Jeannie," she said. She looked at the table. "It looks as though you were expecting me."

He laughed jovially. "There is nearly always an extra guest. I welcome the chance to be hospitable at all times. This is a command of our Lord." His eyes twinkled as he continued. "The more I get into this, the more I realize that Christianity is a people relationship."

She saw compassion in his face as she related her

story. His expression was so gentle and reassuring that she found it easy to talk to him. She began slowly, but soon she was pouring out her heart in words that wouldn't come fast enough.

She explained how she and Barry had become involved in astrology and interested in the doctrine of reincarnation. She told him about Carolyn, the group therapy sessions, and the confrontation with the bishop. Then she told him about their present stress and persecution. When she finished, she looked at his face and saw no evidence of reproof or condemnation.

Brother Raymond knew what had happened, but he also knew that the veil on her understanding had not been completely lifted. What a miracle it was indeed when God delivered a person out of the kingdom of darkness and translated him into the kingdom of His dear Son!

His thoughts rested on biblical truths, truths that he would attempt to share with her. He sought the anointing of the Holy Spirit to reveal these truths to Jeannie. The Holy Spirit alone could put His finger on a cancer and heal it with love and purity. He could remove cancer painlessly, even a cancer of the soul.

Jeannie studied the old minister as he pulled his glasses off and began to clean them. He was a tall, thin man. His face was lined with age but he had a thick head of silver hair. She saw love, humility, meekness, and strength in his face. Something about him made him look as though he had known sorrow; perhaps it was the lines around his eyes. But the smile on his face was genuine and she was certain that if he had known sorrow in the past, he was now peaceful and content. Above all, he seemed very loving and compassionate, and she trusted him immediately.

He began slowly. "Those activities your husband and you have engaged in are forbidden by God, as I'll show you through the scriptures. Seances and things such as that are not of God, and scripture tells us that what is not of God is of the world: Satan's kingdom. There are no two ways about it.

"Barry wants to please God, otherwise he wouldn't have spent the last 12 years as a minister, preaching the Gospel. But I think what's happened to him is exactly what's happened to many Christians, even clergymen: he has allowed himself to be deceived by Satan, because he wasn't thoroughly grounded in the Bible at all times. He became so involved in social matters, in paperwork and counseling his parishioners, in bazaars and other church functions, that he forgot the primary source of his faith: that one-to-one relationship with God that is crucial to the Christian. He was trying to solve other people's problems as well as his own, through his *own* power, and, although he may not have realized it, he was denying God's power."

"It's funny," Jeannie said. "I think I could see that happening all along, yet I didn't realize exactly what was happening, if that makes any sense."

He smiled. "I know what you're trying to say."

"We used to pray all the time, as a family, about little things and big ones. Whenever we had specific problems we went straight to God and handed them over. And we were always happy when we did this." She sighed. "It's my fault. This whole thing is my fault. If I hadn't been so gullible this whole thing wouldn't have happened. He needed me. He became so tired and unhappy, and I was too busy thinking about myself and my own grief and loneliness that I let him fall right into Carolyn's trap."

"Don't heap condemnation upon yourself, Jeannie. That's exactly what Satan wants you to do. He wants you to hate yourself and crawl into a hole somewhere so you'll be no good to anyone. That way he would have one more Christian out of the way. He moved in on Barry when Barry was ripe for the picking."

"But Barry is a good man! He has always put other people first and has been a good father and husband...."

"Yes, Jeannie, and the mayor of this town is a good mayor, and the president of this country is a good president. But God wants us to lean on Him, to depend on Him just as a little child depends on his father. He wants our faith and trust. He wants us to be empty vessels so that He can fill us with His power, His love. I could run around doing good things all day long but if I didn't know Jesus personally and have His love, I would be nothing. I would wear myself out and wither away like the grass. But the Word of the Lord endures forever! Setting our eyes on the people and things around us will only bring us disappointment — haven't you seen that in your own life?" he asked her gently.

"It seems like the past few months have been nothing but one big disappointment. A nightmare." She stood up and walked over to the window. "How can you possibly stay afloat when there's so much ugliness around?"

"By keeping your eyes right on Jesus," the minister answered simply. "By keeping the channels open all the time. Staying in contact with Jesus is somewhat like talking to a friend on the telephone. It's a two-way conversation. God talks to you through His Word, the Bible, and by speaking to your heart. And you talk back to Him, too! The only difference in this phone call is that you're the only one who will hang up the phone and end the conversation. God will keep right on talking to you and answering your questions. He will show you how to be a part of His kingdom just as long as you want to listen. But as soon as you put that receiver down, He's not going to make you pick it up again. He desires your trust and your attentiveness in what He has to offer you, but He won't force it upon you.

"As for Barry — well, God's allowed him to make his own moves. Having Jesus alive in you and being a Spirit-filled Christian makes all the difference in the world!"

Jeannie turned around slowly. "That's exactly what my friend Loretta was telling me recently. You should see how it's changed her life. She's always been cheerful and pleasant, but now she seems like she's found so much inner joy. It's different somehow."

"That it is," Brother Raymond said, smiling broadly. "You and Barry want God, I know that. Barry has served Him. He turned over his career to Him, in fact. It takes a lot of faith to do that, and it must have taken a lot of faith for you to trust God to lead your husband in his profession!

"God tells us that He will forgive our sins if we confess them before Him and ask Him into our lives as our Savior, and that's a blessing that can't be compared with anything else that we ever experienced.

When I was a young man, I based my whole faith in God on the fact that my sins were forgiven and that I was clean in God's sight. But it took quite a while for me to realize that there was more to my relationship with God than just that. He showed me one day through His Word that I was not allowing Him to be my *Lord*. I was still holding on to parts of my life that I considered to be mine and not His. In other words, I was holding on to my old self instead of lifting every facet of my life up to Him for His perfect will to be fulfilled.

"It's not a sacrifice when you ask God to be your Lord. It's an investment. It doesn't mean you have to pray any harder or try to be perfect — it's just an act of faith, telling God that you want Him to show you how to handle your money, your daily affairs or how to raise your children. He'll give you riches you never thought you could ever have!"

Jeannie surprised him by laughing. "You sound as though you've been talking to Loretta. You two have told me the exact same things!"

Brother Raymond smiled. "It's Jesus, Jeannie. I don't know how long it will take Barry to realize that without God he will only find unhappiness, or perhaps just emptiness. Satan has a way of making the world seem awfully rosy and sweet. Witchcraft, astrology, communication with spirits of the dead, sorcery, reincarnation doctrine — these can be very enticing things. They fascinate and amaze. But Satan's enticements are ploys to separate us from God, because we begin to rely on their power rather than God's.

"Barry was in a state of depression, from what you tell me, when this whole thing started. Had he been waiting on the Lord, seeking His will in all things, he would have recognized instantly that witchcraft and other things such as that lead to self-righteousness, self-love, and self-adoration. It's not for us to judge Carolyn, however, but to set our sights on God and to pray for His saving grace in the whole matter. We must rely on His delivery powers. We shouldn't hate Barry and Carolyn, or condemn them, although we hate *the things they do*, because those things are an abomination to God.''

Jeanie stood silently for a moment, then walked back to her chair.

''I want to know more about what's happened to Barry,'' she said slowly. ''I need to understand what it is we're up against.''

Brother Raymond smiled. ''I was hoping you would say that. Many Christians know very little about these things, but some Christians who are being attacked by Satan need to find out just what it is they're coming up against. God talks a lot about demons and about witches or other demon control in the Bible. Paul said in Ephesians 6:12 that 'we wrestle not against flesh and blood, but against principalities, against powers, against the rulers of the darkness of this world, against spiritual wickedness in high places.' Jeannie, can you recognize Satan?''

She shook her head no, not knowing exactly what he meant.

''Well, it's sometimes hard to recognize him, but the only way we can do it is by the power of the Holy Spirit and His discernment to us. The baptism with the Holy Spirit gives this supernatural power and His understanding comes through the Word of God.'' He leaned over and picked up a worn, leather-bound

Bible and set it in his lap.

"Isn't it a fantastic feat for Satan that he so cleverly convinces people that he doesn't exist? And not only that, but he further convinces them that their enemies are their mother, father, husband or wife! God said to Satan in Ezekiel 28:15,16: 'Thou wast perfect in thy ways from the day that thou wast created, till iniquity was found in thee... I will cast thee as profane out of the mountain of God: and I will destroy thee.'

"Satan continually tries to exalt himself above God, and he tries to use us to usurp God's authority. His nature within us tries to exalt self above God. Jesus, who always existed and who created and laid the foundation of the earth and the heavens with His hands, said that He saw Lucifer fall from the sky. Lucifer was created, as were all the angels, for the purpose of glorifying God. Billy Graham, in his book *Angels: God's Secret Agents*, describes Satan's desire to rule over the heavens through his five 'I wills' as set forth in Isaiah 14:

I will ascend into heaven.
I will exalt my throne above the stars of God.
I will sit also upon the mount of the congregation.
I will ascend above the heights of the clouds.
I will be like the most high.
I... I... I...[1]

"Paul tells us that Satan can transform himself into an angel of light, and Paul says it's no wonder that his ministers, or servants, can also be transformed in the same way, as ministers of righteousness. But Paul cautions us that in the end they will be punished according to their works.

"Jesus's ministry dealt greatly with the casting out of demons," the minister continued, turning to

Luke 8:26-33. "Here it is," he said, and began to read:

> *And they arrived at the country of the Gadarenes,*
> *which is over against Galilee. And when he went forth*
> *to land, there met him out of the city a certain man,*
> *which had devils long time, and ware no clothes, neither*
> *abode in any house, but in the tombs. When he saw*
> *Jesus, he cried out, and fell down before him, and with*
> *a loud voice said, What have I to do with thee, Jesus,*
> *thou Son of God most high? I beseech thee, torment*
> *me not. (For he had commanded the unclean spirit to*
> *come out of the man. For oftentimes it had caught him:*
> *and he was kept bound with chains and in fetters; and*
> *he brake the bands, and was driven of the devil into*
> *the wilderness.) And Jesus asked him, saying, What*
> *is thy name? And he said, Legion: because many devils*
> *were entered into him. And they besought him that he*
> *would not command them to go out into the deep. And*
> *there was there an herd of many swine feeding on the*
> *mountain: and they besought him that he would suffer*
> *them to enter into them. And he suffered them. Then*
> *went the devils out of the man, and entered into the*
> *swine: and the herd ran violently down a steep place*
> *into the lake, and were choked.*

In Acts 16, Luke tells us about a girl with a spirit of divination, a fortuneteller in other words, who made much money for her masters. She followed Paul and Silas for many days crying, 'These men are the servants of the most high God which show unto us the way of salvation.' The girl was trying to link her fortunetelling abilities with God and with Paul's ministry. That's why many fortunetellers light a candle to Mary, the mother of Jesus. They will use certain scriptures in an effort to make themselves seem God-fearing, yet they will ignore other scriptures that vehemently forbid their activities. Even Shakespeare says in *The Merchant of Venice* that Satan uses scripture according to his own purpose!

"Paul turned finally and said to the spirit in the girl, 'I command thee in the name of Jesus Christ to come out of her,' and the spirit came out that very hour. The girl's masters saw that their hope of gain was gone, and so they had Paul and Silas beaten and thrown into jail.

"God is showing us that demons (principalities and evil spirits) are all a part of Satan's kingdom. They do exist and they are powerful! And they often disguise themselves so well that man has no idea of their danger. But Paul was aware of Satan's power through that fortuneteller, and he carried on the work of Jesus by using his authority to cast out demons.

"God draws us a clear picture of Satan in the Bible, and He shows us how Satan tricks man into separation from God through activities such as fortunetelling, witchcraft, and calling up spirits from the dead. God expressly forbids witchcraft in the Bible. In Deuteronomy 18, He hands down this commandment through Moses. I'll read the passage to you from *The Living Bible*. In Deuteronomy 18:9 he says, 'When you arrive in the Promised Land you must be very careful lest you be corrupted by the horrible customs of the nations now living there.' In verses 10 through 14, he tells the children of Israel that God forbids them to 'practice black magic, or call on the evil spirits for aid, or be a fortuneteller, or be a serpent charmer, medium, or wizard, or call forth the spirits of the dead. Anyone doing these things is an object of horror and disgust to the Lord, and it is because the nations do these things that the Lord your God will displace them.'

"Exodus 22:18 says that any sorceress (or witch) should be put to death, and Leviticus 19:31 warns us not to defile ourselves by consulting mediums and wizards."

"I think I've read those scriptures before," Jeannie said, "but they always seemed so foreign and I never related them to my life or thought much about them. But they do seem to describe what has been happening to me."

"That's natural," Brother Raymond said. "When we read things like that, especially in the Old Testament, we're inclined to believe that they pertain to another place and time."

"I know. Until a few months ago, I never took fortunetelling or witchcraft seriously. Now I know that they're still being practiced as seriously as they were in biblical times. The scripture you read mentioned mediums. What exactly are they?"

"A medium is a person through whom communications are sent to the living from the spirits for the dead. Let's look at a case in which men have consulted mediums to call up spirits from the dead."

He picked up the Bible. "In the Old Testament, Saul sought a medium to contact the dead prophet Samuel. He needed consultation about the imminent attack of the Philistines. Saul had turned from God and had been disowned by Him; therefore, he did not have God's counsel. In fact, God had refused to help him at all. The story is related in 1 Samuel 28:7-20. Let's look at it in the *The Living Bible:*

> *Saul then instructed his aides to try to find a medium so that he could ask her what to do, and they found one at Endor. Saul disguised himself by wearing ordinary clothing instead of his royal robes. He went*

to the woman's home at night, accompanied by two of his men.

'I've got to talk to a dead man,' he pleaded. 'Will you bring his spirit up?'

...'Well, whom do you want me to bring up?'

'Bring me Samuel,' Saul replied.

When the woman saw Samuel, she screamed. 'You've deceived me! You are Saul!'

'Don't be frightened!' the king told her. 'What do you see?'

'I see a specter coming up out of the earth,' she said.

'What does he look like?'

'He is an old man wrapped in a robe.'

Saul realized that it was Samuel and bowed low before him.

'Why have you disturbed me by bringing me back?' Samuel asked Saul.

'Because I am in deep trouble,' he replied. 'The Philistines are at war with us, and God has left me and won't reply by prophets or dreams; so I have called for you to ask what to do.'

But Samuel replied, 'Why ask me if the Lord has left you and has become your enemy? He has done just as he said he would and has taken the kingdom from you and given it to your rival, David. All this has come upon you because you did not obey the Lord's instruction when he was so angry with Amalek. What's more, the entire Israeli army will be routed and destroyed by the Philistines tomorrow, and you and your sons will be here with me.'

Saul now fell full length upon the ground paralyzed with fright because of Samuel's words.''

Brother Raymond closed the Bible. ''This sort of thing, calling up spirits from the dead through mediums, is not limited to biblical times, as I'm sure you well know. It's still happening today.'' He walked over to the bookshelf and pulled down a book. According to *Sorcery in America*,[2] James A. Pike and Diane Kennedy wrote a book which tells about Bishop Pike's encounters with mediums. Have you ever heard of him?''

''Yes, but I'm not too familiar with his life story.''

''Dr. Pike had a son, Jim, who committed suicide after having lived the life of a drug addict. Dr. Pike found a medium, Mrs. Ena Twigg, to call up Jim from the dead. It's speculated that Dr. Pike was seeking assurance that he wasn't to blame for his son's death.

''These words came to Dr. Pike through Mrs. Twigg from the dead son: '...I haven't met Jesus. They talk about him — a mystic, a seer, yes, a seer. Oh, but Dad, they don't talk about him as a savior...' Jim described the world he was in as a place where 'someone is making things hang together and develop' and he said that this religion he was experiencing was 'without someone forcing God and Jesus down my throat.'

''Dr. Pike also contacted another medium, Rev. George Dailsey, who had claimed he raised Edgar Cayce, the well-known psychic, and others from the dead. Jim's words through the reverend were: 'Nobody seems to talk about him — Jesus. ...some still seem to be church-minded, and are waiting for a Judgment Day, but these seem to be the unenlightened ones,' and he added that the others were expanding their minds and selves toward more Eastern understanding.

''Dr. Pikes' secretary-assistant, who had collaborated with him in his research into psychic phenomena, committed suicide, and after her death it was claimed that her spirit was quoted in a seance as saying, 'Jesus is just another person... we who are here have to earn the right to go up.'

"So you can see, Jeannie, that the words Dr. Pike received though mediums denied the biblical concept of God and Jesus Christ, whereas Samuel's words to king Saul affirmed the personality of the God of Israel and assured Saul of God's impending judgment!"

The minister paused to pour himself and Jeannie another cup of coffee. He observed Jeannie over his spectacles.

"Am I moving too fast for you?" he asked.

"Not at all," she said. "I'm fascinated. Please go on."

He picked up the Bible. "Let me first read you some scriptures that forbid sorcery, or dealings with familiar spirits, then we'll delve a little deeper into the present and what's going on around us right now."

Jeannie watched him as he thumbed through the Bible. She wished Barry could be here with her now. The old minister's eyes were gentle and he was making such an earnest attempt to make her see, to help her to understand. He seemed to be in no hurry at all as he ran his finger down the page of his well-thumbed copy of *The Living Bible*.

"In Leviticus 20:6 the Lord is talking to Moses. He says, 'I will set my face against anyone who consults mediums and wizards instead of me and I will cut that person off from his people.' Further on in that chapter, in verse 27, the Lord says, 'A medium or a wizard — whether man or woman — shall surely be stoned to death. They have caused their own doom.' God further warns us in Isaiah 8:19, 'So why are you trying to find out the future by consulting witches and mediums? Don't listen to their whisperings and mutterings! Can the living find out the future from the dead? Why not ask your God?''' Brother Raymond closed the Bible and sat back.

"God commands us to go directly to Him for our answers, not to a medium or a fortuneteller. When we consult a fortuneteller or ask a medium to call forth a spirit from the dead, we're relying on some person or power other than God, and that leaves the door wide open for Satan to move right in and give us *his* answers, not God's. Once we quit relying on God, we're treading on dangerous ground.''

"I guess that's what I was doing when I first went to Carolyn,'' Jeannie said slowly. "I was bored and she offered a little excitement, with her trances and fortunetelling and seances. And I guess our group therapy meetings did too. We were trying to solve our own problems without going to God and asking Him what He wanted us to do about them. Things really went haywire. The ouija board and the automatic writing... our lives started falling apart right after that.''

Brother Raymond nodded. "It isn't the ouija board that has the power — it's only a piece of cardboard and plastic. But as soon as we rely on the board, or some other object like a crystal ball, we're opening that door again and Satan will jump in feet first.

"I remember reading about a modern-day witch who practices fortunetelling. She claims to have 400 authentic witches as personal friends, and she estimates the world witch population to be at eight million. She was quoted in a leading newspaper interview as saying that people are searching for a religion in which they don't have to live a godlike life, a religion that acknowledges them as human beings. She told a reporter that she didn't just wake up one morning and discover that she was a witch. According to her, witchcraft is like any other religion; the decision to accept it must be made and accepted consciously, and with maturity.

"Let's talk about fortunetelling. Have you ever heard of Jeane Dixon?"

Jeannie nodded. "I've heard her name linked with astrology mostly."

"That's one of the ways she tells fortunes. She uses crystal balls, cards, and intricate charts. Once she won a Cadillac by picking the right number from 14,000 tickets. She's also been able to recover lost articles through her 'second sight,' predict the outcome of horse races, and discover how magic tricks are performed. Her biographer, Ruth Montgomery, says that Jeane is a person 'extremely sensitive to physic powers,' according to Gordon Lindsay in *Sorcery in America*.[3] Lindsay adds that it is unnecessary for Jeane to go into deep trances to get her revelations, unlike most mediums.

"Lindsay talks about mediums and their apparent power in the supernatural world:

> *The purpose of seducing spirits of course is to deceive and lead people away from the truth of the Scriptures. These spirits indeed have a remarkable knowledge of circumstances occurring in people's lives and they have the power to impersonate the voices of those who have passed on. People ignorant of the nature of the spirits are quickly deceived by any preternatural phenomenon, and once persuaded of its authenticity may be led from delusion to delusion until they will commit the most irrational acts."*[4]

"Didn't Mrs. Dixon predict the coming of the antichrist?" Jeannie asked. "I read somewhere that she predicted that he would come some time in this century."

"Yes, in a way. As you know, the book of Revelation in the Bible talks about the antichrist, the Son of Perdition, who will wage war against Christianity and put on a facade of peace and brotherhood. Mrs. Dixon predicts: 'Mankind will begin to feel the great force of this man about 1980 and his power will grow mightily until 1999, when there will be peace on earth to all men of good will.' Lindsay comments on this prediction:

> In the case of Mrs. Dixon, her prophecies of the coming of a superman to solve the world's difficulties and to bring peace to the earth in the latter part of the century has indeed sombre implications. The Bible clearly speaks of the coming of the antichrist at the end of the age, who achieves great power in the earth and then uses it in a merciless campaign to wipe out Christianity and to usurp worship to himself. Mrs. Dixon predicts from a vision she had the rise of this superman, not as the antichrist as the Bible reveals, but as God's gift to the world to usher in a new Christianity and to restore peace to the nations. The real danger of Mrs. Dixon's prediction is that it is helping to pave the way for Satan to introduce his final masterpiece of delusion. Unwittingly she is preparing people to accept this mighty personage as the world's saviour. Nothing is said about Christ and His appearing which is the true hope of the church, but that this great man will arise who will solve the world's problems, introduce a new Christianity, and bring peace to the earth by the year 1999 A.D....
>
> What is the significance of Jeane Dixon's vision? The significance is that her messiah is none other than the antichrist, The Man of Sin, the Son of Perdition

*who will force men to take the mark of the beast, ere
they can buy or sell and who will wage relentless war
against Christianity.* (Rev. 13:4-8.)[5]

"Lindsay adds that this vision of Mrs. Dixon's
came from a serpent, and he says that this must certainly be ample proof that her vision was Satan-
inspired, since the serpent was the creature who also
brought sin into the world."

Mary entered the room with their lunch. Jeannie
jumped up to help her set the food on the table. She
and Brother Raymond sat across from each other at
the small wooden table in a corner of the room.

The old minister bowed his head. "Father, thank
You for this nourishment for our bodies. And we
thank You, Jesus, for this time together and for what
You're going to do in Barry's life, and in Jeannie's.
Amen."

"Amen," she echoed.

They ate in silence for a few minutes. Jeannie felt
more relaxed than she had in a long time. Her teacher
had spoken authoritatively about the occult. He read
the scriptures in a tone that made her know that he
didn't take them lightly, yet she knew he wasn't condemning Carolyn or Barry or anyone else; he was
only emphasizing God's commandments and view of
activities such as witchcraft. She knew that if Barry
walked through the door right now, Brother
Raymond would invite him to share his lunch with
him, just as he had taken her in without a second
thought. He wasn't condescending in the least; he
treated her as though she were very important and he
taught her things in such a way that she didn't feel
ignorant or embarrassed to ask about any subject.

"What about astrology and horoscopes?" she

asked him. "I see people every day referring to charts and listings of all kinds, even in the daily newspapers."

Brother Raymond shook his head slowly. "It all looks very innocent, doesn't it? But astrology is definitely linked with sorcery, according to the Bible." He picked up *The Living Bible.* "Isaiah 47:10 talks specifically about astrology and stargazing: 'Your "wisdom" and "knowledge" have caused you to turn away from me and claim that you yourself are Jehovah.' In verses 13-14 God says, 'You have advisers by the ton — your astrologers and stargazers, who try to tell you what the future holds. But they are as useless as dried grass burning in the fire. They cannot even deliver themselves! You'll get no help from them at all. Theirs is no fire to sit beside to make you warm!' "

"That passage is in Isaiah?" Jeannie asked him. "Then that means people were consulting astrologers and stargazers before Christ's time. I don't think I ever realized that the practice went back that far."

"Oh yes. Gordon Lindsay talks about the origins of astrology, or stargazing, in the book I showed you.[6] He explains that in early ages men realized that their everyday lives were affected by what was occurring in the heavens. The sun and rain gave them productive harvests, and storms and things such as that could wipe out their whole production of crops. So the Babylonians believed that powerful gods sat in the heavens.

"Priests, in their demonic rites, perfected a theory in which all things which occurred on earth were the result of the various phenomena observed in the heavens. They assumed that each planet represented a god who had power so great that he could control the lives of people on earth. Twelve of the constellations supposedly ruled the 12 months of the year. They began to make intricate charts relating to the time of birth of a person and from these they cast the horoscopes.

"According to Lindsay, the prophecy in Isaiah 47 is directed particularly at Babylon, the nation which birthed the art of astrology. That chapter I read to you definitely links astrology and prognostication with sorcery! The Kings of Babylon would ask the stargazers for instructions about when to go to war or engage in other activities. This prophecy declared that 'the multitude of thy sorceries' could not save Babylon, and that astrologers and stargazers would eventually be judged and receive retribution for their activities, together with Babylon. And that's exactly what happened!

"Lindsay says that at the hour of Babylon's judgment, Belshazzar, the king, and his ladies and lords were in the midst of a profane feast. They suddenly saw the hand of a man writing on the wall. They summoned the astrologers to interpret the meaning of the strange handwriting, but the astrologers didn't know what it meant. Daniel, the prophet, was the only one who could interpret the message on the wall, the message that spelled the doom of Babylon. So it was a man whose wisdom came from God and the scriptures who could deal with this phenomenon, not the stargazers. Their wisdom was no good when a real crisis arose."

The old teacher buttered his bread slowly. "I don't think God condemns man or punishes him for being curious, Jeannie. We're curious creatures, all of us. We naturally want to know what the moon looks like up close, or what causes an eclipse, or why snow falls. Man has always studied the heavens; it's a big part of his life on earth. But having a dependence upon man's calculations to guide our moves — that separates us from God. By consulting charts that tell us whether we should take a certain job or enter into a particular business venture, we're cutting off our trust in God and putting it in something that springs from man. God desires our trust in Him. He wants us to depend on Him from day to day, and He blesses us immensely for our faith. The more childlike and trusting we are toward Him, the more He can do for us.

"God always tells the truth; Satan never tells the truth for long. Lindsay has sometimes checked the fulfillment of prophecies of noted astrologers. Hollywood's favorite astrologer, Norville, made six predictions in *Look* magazine in November of 1939. Not one of these six predictions proved correct! Would you like to read those predictions and their outcomes?"

"Yes, I would. It sounds interesting."

The old man picked up Gordon Lindsay's *Sorcery in America* and found the page. Jeannie began to read the predictions and their outcome:

> In a matter of months Hitler will meet a tragic fate. Death may come to him from an assassin, or by a battle wound in the throat or heart region, or even by suicide. His end will be sudden and violent amid confusion. (Actually Hitler lived another 5 years to throw the whole world into a convulsion.)

> In Spring of 1940 is the period of worst affliction in Hitler's chart. But in any event he cannot survive the year. His successor — Goering — will find the

German people growing more restless and finally attempting a revolt against him. (Instead of Hitler's being overthrown, the spring of 1940 was the period of his greatest success — the overrunning in succession of Denmark, Norway, Holland, Belgium, and France.)

For England and France, victory is clearly indicated. They will blockade and finally starve Germany. With the Maginot Line as an impregnable barrier, they will invade German territory weakening Germany and at last shattering her morale. (What actually happened was that the impregnable Maginot Line was flanked in the matter of hours. France fell and spent four years under the iron heel of the invader.)

Mussolini will disagree with Hitler and ultimately sell out to the democracies for territorial concessions. (Wrong again. Mussolini threw in his lot with Hitler. Years later he died an ignominious death at the hand of angry partisans. Territory that Mussolini had seized from other nations was retored to their owners.)

And Poland and Czechoslovakia will be restored with additional territory. (Not true, Russia connived with Hitler to carve up Poland. After the war these two nations became Soviet satellites.)

Astrologically the trend is definitely toward a Republican victory in 1940. (Still wrong. Wendell Wilkie was defeated and Franklin Roosevelt was re-elected for a third term.)[7]

"These are Lindsay's observations," the teacher said.

Mary entered the room again to take their plates and motioned for Jeannie to sit back down when she arose to help. The housekeeper smiled and left the room quickly.

Brother Raymond leaned back, stretched his arms out and took a deep breath.

"How about a walk?" he asked. "I think we could use some fresh air."

Jeannie nodded.

The old minister walked over to a closet and took out an umbrella as Jeannie put her sweater on.

"Do you have a vegetable garden?" he asked suddenly.

"No, I have more success with flowers," she answered.

"I'll be right back," he said, smiling. He left the room and returned a few minutes later. He was carrying a large bushel basket. "Let's go find your dinner," he said, his eyes twinkling.

Indeed, if a man should live many years, let him rejoice in them all, and let him remember the days of darkness, for they shall be many. Everything that is to come will be futility.

Ecclesiastes 11:8 NASB

16
KIDNAPPED?

Loretta was sitting on the front porch reading and watching the children play hide-and-seek when Barry drove up in his car. She stood up as he got out of the car and walked toward her. He looked older than he had when she had last seen him early in the summer.

"Hello, Loretta," he said, stopping several feet away from her. "Jeannie asked me to pick up the children. She's going to be delayed."

Before she could answer, Barry called Mary and Charles and they ran to him breathless and excited, and began to tell him about the Walt Disney movie they had seen that morning.

Barry thanked Loretta and said good-bye as he ushered the children to the car. Loretta started to ask him if he would have Jeannie call her when he got home, but she decided against it because Barry seemed to be in a hurry.

She waved to the kids as the car pulled away, then picked up her book and resumed her reading.

For our struggle is not against flesh and blood, but against the rulers, against the powers, against the world forces of this darkness, against the spiritual forces of wickedness in the heavenly places.

Ephesians 6:12 NASB

17
TRAVELING BACK IN TIME

Jeannie followed Brother Raymond through the rear door of the church and out into the large yard in the back. She shivered slightly as the cool air hit her, and she wondered how he was going to take her vegetable picking when winter was so close at hand.

They walked around what was apparently the minister's living quarters and Jeannie saw a large greenhouse in front of them.

"I think you'll enjoy this," he said.

They entered the greenhouse and Jeannie was surprised at what she saw inside. There were vines climbing everywhere, laden with large, ripe tomatoes, and there were other plants growing in neat rows. They walked past large fiberglass containers that were filled with a gravel-like substance from which the plants were growing.

"This is a hydroponic garden," he said. "The solution at the bottom of these containers consists of vitamins and minerals, which sustain the plants instead of natural soil."

"Do the vegetables taste any different?" she asked.

"Oh, some say they do. Mary and I keep a vegetable garden outside during the summer, too, but it's very nice to be able to provide our church members and ourselves with home-grown vegetables year 'round."

A young boy appeared at the back of the

greenhouse. He looked shyly at Jeannie.

"Timmy, I want you to meet Jeannie," the minister said. He turned to her. "Timmy keeps this greenhouse running like a top. He wants to have his own hydroponic garden someday, when he gets out of college. Right, Timmy?"

"Right, Brother Raymond." Timmy grinned broadly, and Jeannie could tell by the look on his face that he and the minister were very close.

The boy left after a few minutes and they walked slowly past the rows of plants.

"Brother Raymond, I realize I've taken up much of your time, but may I ask one more question? I saw automatic writing work and I witnessed table lifting. These things really happened right before our eyes. Who can deny their reality?"

"No one who has seen them," he replied. "There is definitely an unseen world right at our fingertips, and Satan is the prince of this world. When Jesus was fasting, Satan came to Him and said that he would give Him everything in the world if He would bow down and worship him. Jesus answered, 'Get thee hence, Satan: for it is written, Thou shalt worship the Lord thy God, and him only shalt thou serve.' But the interesting thing is this: Jesus did not deny that Satan had control of this world! As John Milton wrote in Paradise Lost, 'Millions of spiritual creatures walk the earth unseen, both when we wake and when we sleep.'"

"I've read books about Edgar Cayce," she said. "He was such a good man, devoting much of his life to healing and reading the Bible. Didn't he have psychic powers?"

"Yes, he did. Gordon Lindsay includes Cayce's

case history.

"Edgar's psychic experiences began at a very early age. His grandfather, a psychic, was a dowser who was able to locate water with a branch of hazel. According to Gordon Lindsay, information about Grandfather Cayce is related in Joseph Millard's book, *Edgar Cayce Mystery Man of Miracles*.[1] The grandfather could make tables rise by holding his hands over them, or he could concentrate on a broom and cause it to stand up and dance around the room by itself.

"Millard says that when Edgar's grandfather was killed in a horseback riding accident, his psychic powers were apparently transferred to Edgar, who was a boy at the time. Edgar suffered a spinal injury one day and his once quiet behavior became unruly. He began hanging out with wild crowds. One day when he was a young man, he suddenly lost his voice and had blinding headaches and amnesia. He was found in a town 40 miles away by a neighbor. Doctors tried to cure him and a hypnotist tried to bring him around by post-hypnotic suggestion, but nothing worked.

"Then Cayce tried to hypnotize himself, and it worked. His voice returned to normal. He was able to diagnose his case and from that time on he decided to use this power to diagnose others' illnesses, and he was successful. He did all this in trances, and in most cases his diagnoses were correct and the patient was cured. He was also clairvoyant and gave readings for people hundreds of miles away. But, according to Millard, Cayce was afraid of his power. He was afraid he might be using the devil's power in disguise, because he sensed evil forces in his life. His own family suffered sicknesses over which he had no control, and 'the lying spirit that controlled him promised healing in his own life two days before his death.'

"God warns us in 2 Corinthians 11:14 of the *New American Standard Bible:* 'And no wonder, for even Satan disguises himself as an angel of light.' Now, Jeannie, compare the force that controlled Cayce's life with the force that is the Holy Spirit. The Holy Spirit never intrudes or pushes relentlessly. He teaches, prompts, and leads us gently, never taking control, yet He's always there when we need Him. We are far from being puppets when we ask for His help and guidance. If these evil forces had not gained supremacy in Cayce's life, and if the true light of the scriptures had been revealed to him, he probably would have been used by God in great crusades. Imagine the possibilities!

"The doctrine of reincarnation and Cayce's supportive view of astrology are both forbidden in the Scriptures."

They walked back to Brother Raymond's office.

"Millard says that Cayce was asked once if the planets have anything to do with ruling the destiny of man. Cayce replied affirmatively. Let me read it to you:

> 'They do. The inclination of man is ruled by the planets under which he is born. In this way the destiny of man lies within the sphere of the scope of the planets. With the given position of the solar system at the time of the birth of the individual, it can be worked out — that is, the inclinations and actions, without the will power taken into consideration.'[2]

"The spirit controlling Cayce endorsed reincarnation. Cayce was horrified that this doctrine did not go along with the Bible. A student of the occult and science calmed his horror by pointing out the scripture in which Jesus said, 'Except a man be born again he cannot see the kingdom of God.' The spirits will pervert God's words in an effort to prove the theory of reincarnation, yet Jesus clearly stated that the idea of a physical birth or rebirth was erroneous.

"An example of how impersonating spirits work to try to prove reincarnation is recorded in Lindsay's book. It is about a boy living in Jerusalem who, it is claimed, lived 3,000 years ago as King David. The story is truly fascinating. I'd like you to hear it as it is written here:

> The name of this young boy is David Morris. He was born in 1961, the son of a dental surgeon. At times the boy has strange trances, and when under these spells speaks in an odd variation of the Hebrew language. The boy's father on one occasion recorded what he was saying on tape and took it to the National Museum in Jerusalem. At the museum he played the tape for Dr. Zvi Hermann, acting curator of the Ancient Manuscripts section, who specialized in deciphering old manuscripts. When he heard the tape, he perceived that the words were in ancient Hebrew. Since the father had not informed the curator that they had been spoken by the boy, the latter supposed that the tape had been made by a professional actor rehearsing a part in a play, and he was incredulous when he heard the truth. Part of what he translated from the tape was as follows:
>
> 'This is the king speaking to his people. Follow me and I shall lead you to glory. I have built the temple of the Lord. Beware you sinners and weak-hearted ones. This is the house of God. No one dares enter it in a spirit of pride and vanity. Rally to me and the Lord will lead us to eternal greatness.'
>
> The father had been an agnostic who even doubted the existence of God. But when the curator interpreted the words, he became convinced that reincarnation was

a fact and that the boy was actually the spirit of King David. Mr. Morris retained the services of a psychiatrist to observe his son and to record what he said over an extended period of time. They took the lad to Mt. Zion where King David is buried. The lad went into a trance and spoke for 20 minutes. Translated, it was an exhortation to the people of Israel to seize the site of the Holy Temple from the Arabs. Translated he said.

'My soul suffers mortal anguish each time I hear the infidels, (The Muezzin) calling from the House of God I have built. Destroy them with sword and with fire, for the Lord is with us.'

The psychiatrist came to the conclusion that the child probably had heard things about King David and had absorbed them subconsciously. But the father knew this was not the answer. When the boy came out of a trance, he knew nothing about what he said. Some kind of spirit had taken control and caused him to say these things.

May 15, 1967, the 19th anniversary of Israel's independence was celebrated in Jerusalem. 'Take me to Mt. Zion,' the boy begged his father. As they entered the arched entrance to David's tomb, the lad went into a trance. 'Victory! Victory!' he cried. 'Do not despair, my people, and victory will be ours. We shall build a new house of God and I shall lead you to everlasting glory.'

Within 24 hours the armed forces of four Arab nations moved to besiege Israel's frontiers. The father, Dr. Morris, was called to active duty.

On June 4, the day before the war started, the child again went into a trance. 'Seize the ridge!' he cried, 'Protect your right flank. Advance! Advance! The enemy is breaking. He is fleeing now. Do not let him escape. Surround! Destroy! Annihilate!'

The next day early in the morning the war broke out and the little nation of Israel surrounded on all sides, sent forth her armies against vastly superior forces and in six days had pushed forward to the Suez Canal to the South and to the Jordan River on the East.[3]

"The child said many other things while he was in these trances, and many people in Jerusalem were convinced that this child was actually the living reincarnation of the King David, who lived nearly 3,000 years ago. The boy was only in the first grade when this book was written, and he knew nothing of all these things. Yet when he would go into a trance, he would speak many stange things, like the ones I've read to you and he would tell those who listened to him to prepare themselves for another war. Of course many orthodox religious circles are amazed at this phenomenon, but they refuse to take a stand on the issue.

"Rabbi Yedida Cohen of the Supreme Religious Council commented on this phenomenon: 'We cannot admit anything openly because the Jewish faith is based on the theory that King David is the Messiah, and when he returns to earth the Kingdom of God will prevail. This means resurrection of the dead and other things such as eternal justice, immortality, and the like. I don't think the world, mankind, or even we Israelis are ripe for it yet. But,' he added, 'if the boy is not the Messiah he cannot be King David — provided one believes in reincarnation.' "

"That's amazing," Jeannie said. "There really is a power then — a psychic power."

"That's right," Brother Raymond replied. "Some people believe that spirits can take possession of people and have an amazing ability to impersonate or disguise themselves as historical figures as in this case, or, in the case of Dr. Pike, as a dead loved one (his son Jim).

"It's easy to see how this could happen. Since spirits are not mortal, they do not die when the body they inhabit dies — they just enter someone else instead. Everlasting spirits can control a human mind. The demoniac freed by Jesus was 'clothed and in his right mind.' Suppose for a minute that an evil spirit had indwelt Dr. Pike's son — wouldn't that spirit know everything about him? We have no way of knowing that Dr. Pike ever communicated with the real Jim at all. My theory is that Jim's own spirit was elsewhere, and that what Dr. Pike was communicating with was an evil spirit.

"In the same way, when people 'remember' past lives, I believe these 'memories' are fed into their minds by evil spirits — spirits who lived in or near the people whose reincarnations they simulate. Since spirits are immortal, each evil spirit could have a minutely detailed knowledge about thousands of generations of people, as well as of the lives of people who had been closely connected with those they had indwelt.

"Yes, there are definitely unseen powers and they're not to be trifled with. As I've shown you through the scriptures, God forbids us to draw on these powers, because he knows that without the power of the Holy Spirit we don't have the armor to fight the power of Satan. We are given power by God and the authority of Jesus to bind Satan and cast demons out of individuals.

"The Bible tells us that the righteous man will be at home with the Lord after death. In the story of Lazarus and the rich man, God would not let either of them return to earth after they had died to preach repentance to those who were still on earth. Lazarus went to heaven to be with Abraham, and the rich man went to hell. Those were to be their permanent homes, evidently, because they were not permitted to return to earth as spirits of the dead. God knew that it would come to no good if the spirits of the dead returned to earth. Reincarnation does not line up with the Bible; and the return of spirits from the dead to communicate with those of us on earth is forbidden by God. Evil spirits, fallen angels, can communicate with people on earth, but the spirits of the dead humans cannot.

''There are so many illustrations and scripture references dealing with things like this that it would be impossible and even unfair to burden you with them all in one afternoon.

''You may want to read Agnes Sanford's autobiography, *Sealed Orders*.[4] The book tells the story of Agnes, a young daughter of missionary parents in China, who entered a Buddhist temple one day. She folded her hands together and bowed before the idol and said '*o-me-to-fu*' as she had seen the monks do when they worshipped. As time passed she came to believe that everyone had two voices within them that contradicted each other. Because of episodes like this, it is very dangerous to practice T.M. or yoga, or other things of that nature which stem from one of the eastern religions. They draw man away from prayer as God originally intended it to be in the Bible, and may make him worship, in a sense, either himself or the world around him, instead of God. Agnes chose Jesus as the Ruler of her life and was not caught in the deceitful clutches of the devil.

''The ancient deceiver, Satan himself, counterfeits every high and pure law of God, and that includes prayer. When we, as Christians, pray to

God in this unknown tongue, that is through the power of the Holy Spirit, our prayers are lifted up in the perfect will of God. Paul tells us in Romans 8:26-27 of *The Living Bible:* 'And in the same way — by our faith — the Holy Spirit helps us with our daily problems and in our praying. For we don't even know what we should pray for, nor how to pray as we should; but the Holy Spirit prays for us with such feeling that it cannot be expressed in words. And the Father who knows all hearts knows, of course, what the Spirit is saying as he pleads for us in harmony with God's own will.'

''Chanting in Sanskrit is actually a translation of praise to a god, also. However, it is not done through the Holy Spirit, which means that chanting in this way is not praise or worship in the way that God intended when He sent us the Holy Spirit, the divine intercessor, to help us pray. Therefore if a person chants without the aid of the Holy Spirit, he may be praying to the god of this present world — as 2 Corinthians 4 calls Satan. It's true that Satan will give a temporary peace, but then he will reward his servants the way he rewarded Edgar Cayce, with sickness and death. The positions in yoga, for example, are seemingly innocent exercises, yet they open the mind to evil spirits, rather than God's Spirit.

The transcendental meditator practices his meditation for 20-minute periods twice a day. Paul, on the other hand, exhorts the Christian to rejoice evermore! To pray without ceasing! To give thanks in everything!

''The Living Word, the Lamb of God, is returning soon for His bride. He created the heavens and the earth with His hands and will one day fold them up as a garment and they will be changed. But He never changes, Jeannie. He always remains the same. He doesn't disguise Himself as Satan does, because He doesn't need to. He doesn't force Himself on us because He wants us to come to Him because we want what He has to offer: peace, love, and pure joy!'' Brother Raymond leaned forward, his face beaming with excitement. "We glory in the beautiful works of His creation, but we worship the Creator, and not the creation!

"Reincarnation, the doctrine of devils, distorts many of God's natural, active laws, and it denies the whole plan of salvation through Jesus. The Bible tells us that we're washed by the blood of Jesus, who forgave our sins so that we might have everlasting life. We can enter the kingdom of God right here and now, by believing and by repenting for our sins. We don't need to climb any 'spiritual ladders' or work a lifetime in an effort to reach a higher plane.

"Suppose a man owns a piece of land. He's poor, and he works hard for many years just to stay alive and feed his family. One day, as he is working strenuously on this piece of land, he discovers oil, and he is suddenly very wealthy. He rejoices at his new-found wealth, and he is jubilant. But what he doesn't realize is that he was always wealthy — that oil was lying there in the ground all the time. The man just didn't know it and wasn't utilizing what was there all along."

Brother Raymond smiled. "That wealth, that joy and peace and love, that net full of fish is there, waiting for us all to discover it. We have great wealth just sitting there at our fingertips, if we'll only ask for it. God wants us to be happy, and He wants to share the riches of His kingdom with us. 'Have faith in God,' Jesus tells us in Mark 11:22-23: 'For verily I say unto you, That whosoever shall say unto this mountain, Be thou removed, and be thou cast into the sea; and shall not doubt in his heart, but shall believe that those things which he saith shall come to pass; he shall have whatsoever he saith.' He wants our faith, Jeannie. That's why He said in verse 24: 'What things soever ye desire, when ye pray, believe that ye receive them, and ye shall have them.'

"The law of sowing and reaping is bountifully present in our lives. Compare E.S.P., which is Satan's counterfeit, with faithful prayer. You can choose to go to Satan and his fallen angels will talk with you; or you can go to God, and his Spirit will talk with you. God can deliver His word by His holy angels if He chooses this way of speaking to us. By choosing the method, you choose whom you will serve and who will serve you. 'Are they not all ministering spirits, sent forth to minister for them who shall be heirs of salvation?' asks the writer of Hebrews 1:14.

"A man goes into a trance and Satan speaks through him. A man of God gives a prophecy, and the Holy Spirit gives a message through him."

The sound of teacups rattling against saucers was heard as the housekeeper entered the room, pushing a cart laden with a delicate splendor of pastries.

"Ah, Mary, you've done it again," the minister said to her. "They look delicious!" He turned to Jeannie. " I wouldn't think of letting you leave without dessert, physically or spiritually." The twinkle in his eye told Jeannie that the best part of the conversation was yet to come.

Let love of the brethren continue.
Do not neglect to show hospitality to strangers, for by
this some have entertained angels without knowing it.

Hebrews 13:1-2 NASB

18

ENTERTAINING ANGELS UNAWARES

Jeannie gazed out the large window of Brother Raymond's library. The gray and white of the rainy afternoon enfolded her and the old minister, wrapping them in thoughts both pensive and sobering. They sat in silence for a few minutes as Mary came in and out, refilling their cups with coffee and clearing away the last dishes.

"It's appropriate that we're having dessert now," the minister said, as he wiped his glasses with a napkin. "Its sweetness enhances the ending of our conversation with flavor and gladness, doesn't it? Because as wretchedly as Satan has ruled this universe since Adam's fall, leaving indelible marks of crime, disease, pestilence, and war, even greater is God's protection and rule with His myriads of angels. First John 4:4 says: 'Ye are of God, little children, and have overcome them: because greater is he that is in you, than he that is in the world.' Satan left God's holy domain with one-third of the angels, but God kept two-thirds for His holy purposes.

"Billy Graham opens his book *Angels: God's Secret Agents* with several fascinating accounts. I'd like you to hear some of them." The minister opened a book and put his glasses on. "Graham writes:

> My wife, who was born and raised in China,
> recalls that in her childhood days tigers lived in the

mountains. One day a poor woman went up to the foothills to cut grass. To her back was tied a baby, and a little child walked beside her. In her hand she carried a sickle to cut grass. Just as she reached the top of the hill she heard a roar. Frightened almost speechless she looked around to see a mother tigress springing at her, followed by two cubs. This illiterate Chinese mother had never attended school or entered a church. She had never seen a Bible. But a year or two earlier a missionary had told her about Jesus, 'who is able to help you when you are in trouble.' As the claws of the tigress tore her arm and shoulder, the woman cried out in a frenzy, 'Oh Jesus, help me!' This ferocious beast, instead of attacking again to get an easy meal, suddenly turned and ran away.

The Bible says, 'He will give his angels charge of you, to guard you in all your ways' (Psalm 91:11 RSV). Had God sent an angel to protect this poor ignorant Chinese woman? Are there supernatural beings today who are able to influence the affairs of men and nations?

Dr. S.W. Mitchell, a celebrated Philadelphia neurologist, had gone to bed after an exceptionally tiring day. Suddenly he was awakened by someone knocking on his door. Opening it he found a little girl, poorly dressed and deeply upset. She told him her mother was very sick and asked him if he would please come with her. It was a bitterly cold, snowy night, but though he was bone tired, Dr. Mitchell dressed and followed the girl.

*As **Reader's Digest** reports the story, he found the mother desperately ill with pneumonia. After arranging for medical care, he complimented the sick woman on the intelligence and persistence of her little daughter. The woman looked at him strangely and then said, 'My daughter died a month ago.' She added, 'Her shoes and coat are in the clothes closet there.' Dr. Mitchell, amazed and perplexed, went to the closet and opened the door. There hung the very coat worn by the little girl who had brought him to tend to her mother.*

It was warm and dry and could not possibly have been out in the wintry night.

Could the doctor have been called in the hour of desperate need by an angel who appeared as this woman's young daughter? Was this the work of God's angels on behalf of the sick woman?

The Reverend John G. Paton, a missionary in the New Hebrides Island, tells a thrilling story involving the protective care of angels. Hostile natives surrounded his mission headquarters one night, intent on burning the Patons out and killing them. John Paton and his wife prayed all during that terror-filled night that God would deliver them. When daylight came they were amazed to see the attackers unaccountably leave. They thanked God for delivering them.

A year later, the chief of the tribe was converted to Jesus Christ, and Mr. Paton, remembering what had happened, asked the chief what had kept him and his men from burning down the house and killing them. The chief replied in surprise, 'Who were all those men you had with you there?' The missionary answered, 'There were no men there; just my wife and I.' The chief argued that they had seen many men standing guard — hundreds of big men in shining garments with drawn swords in their hands. They seemed to circle the mission station so that the natives were afraid to attack. Only then did Mr. Paton realize that God had sent His angels to protect them...

A Persian colporteur was accosted by a man who asked him if he had a right to sell Bibles. 'Why, yes,' he answered, 'we are allowed to sell these books anywhere in the country!' The man looked puzzled, and asked, 'How is it, then, that you are always surrounded by soldiers? I planned three times to attack you, and each time, seeing the soldiers I left you alone. Now I no longer want to harm you.' Were these soldiers heavenly beings?[1]

"What are your impressions, Jeannie? Do you attribute these incidents to 'Lady Luck' or to the emotionalism of the unstable under stress? Or do you believe it's possible that angels were sent to help these people?''

''Until I began to see Satan ravage destruction in our lives, I didn't believe in his existence. You asked me when I first got here if I could recognize Satan, and I know now that I never could, because I had never acknowledged the fact that Satan is alive and well! Yes, I find it not only feasible but perfectly delightful to believe in the existence of angels. The story about the little girl intrigues me. Do they appear in physical form, or are they usually invisible?''

''Angels don't possess physical bodies, but they do have the ability to change their appearance. Daniel sensed the presence of an angel, invisible to human eyes, in the lions' den when he said, 'My God hath sent his angel, and hath shut the lions' mouths;' Mary, the mother of Jesus, and Mary Magdalene beheld the dazzling angel who easily rolled away the heavy stone from the tomb of Jesus; and Abraham, Lot and Jacob recognized angels when they appeared in physical form.

''The Hebrew children — Shadrach, Meshach, and Abednego — were thrown into a furnace of blazing fire because they would not serve the gods of Nebuchadnezzar or worship the golden image he had set up. The fire had no effect upon them — they came out of the furnace completely unharmed, and the king himself admitted that God had sent His angel to deliver His servants who put their trust in Him.

''Graham says that angels are amazing creatures who have an 'exotic beauty completely foreign to human conception,' and he adds that they are exempt from disease, age, and death, according to the Bible. They have no need for redemption, as does man, since they continued in obedience and have never fallen from God's grace.

"In *The Living Bible*, Hebrews 13:2 tells us not to forget to be kind to strangers, 'for some who have done this have entertained angels without realizing it!' That's really something to think about, isn't it? Psalm 91:11,12 tells us that God 'orders his angels to protect you wherever you go. They will steady you with their hands to keep you from stumbling against the rocks on the trail.' And the psalmist adds in verse 13 that 'you can safely meet a lion or step on poisonous snakes, yes, even trample them beneath your feet!'

"Graham says that the new fear and intrigue of demonic forces and interest in the occult would not be nearly as widespread if people recognized the power and protection of angelic beings.

"Psalm 91 tells us that God gives His angels charge over us, and that they guard us in all our ways, lest we strike our feet against stones. Some say that's like a Christian's insurance policy!

"Corrie ten Boom writes of the angelic protection she experienced at the Nazi Ravensbruck prison camp:

> *'Together we entered the terrifying building. At a table were women who took away all our possessions. Everyone had to undress completely and then go to a room where her hair was checked.*
>
> *'I asked a woman who was busy checking the possessions of the new arrivals if I might use the toilet. She pointed to a door, and I discovered that the convenience was nothing more that a hole in the shower-room floor. Betsie stayed close beside me all the time. Suddenly I had an inspiration. "Quick, take off your*

woolen underwear,'' I whispered to her. I rolled it up
with mine and laid the bundle in a corner with my little
Bible. The spot was alive with cockroaches, but I didn't
worry about that. I felt wonderfully relieved and happy.
''The Lord is busy answering our prayers, Betsie,'' I
whispered. ''We shall not have to make the sacrifice
of all our clothes.''

'We hurried back to the row of women waiting to
be undressed. A little later, after we had had our
showers and put on our shirts and shabby dresses, I
hid the roll of underwear and my Bible under my dress.
It did bulge out obviously through my dress; but I
prayed, ''Lord, cause now thine angels to surround me;
and let them not be transparent today, for the guards
must not see me.'' I felt perfectly at ease. Calmly I
passed the guards. Everyone was checked, from the
front, the sides, the back. Not a bulge escaped the eyes
of the guard. The woman just in front of me had hidden
a woolen vest under her dress; it was taken from her.
They let me pass, for they did not see me. Betsie, right
behind me, was searched.

'But outside awaited another danger. On each side
of the door were women who looked everyone over for
a second time. They felt over the body of each one who
passed. I knew they would not see me, for the angels
were still surrounding me. I was not even surprised
when they passed me by, but within me rose the jubilant
cry, ''Oh Lord, if Thou dost so answer prayer, I can
face even Ravensbruck unafraid.''[2]

''Well, Jeannie, I have a couple more stories I'd
like you to read, if you have time. I'd like you to read
one specific passage from *Angels: God's Secret Agents*
by Billy Graham. It applies specifically to you, I feel,
in your search for peace and understanding. I think it
might give you some perspective on the forces you've
come up against.''

''I'd like very much to read it,'' she said, taking
the book from him. She began to read.

The Scriptures are full of dramatic evidences of the protective care of angels in their earthly services to the people of God. Paul admonished Christians to put on all the armor of God that they may stand firmly in the face of evil (Ephesians 6:10-12). Our struggle is not against flesh and blood (physical powers alone), but against the spiritual (superhuman) forces of wickedness in heavenly spheres. Satan, the prince of the power of the air, promotes a ''religion'' but not true faith; he promotes false prophets. So the powers of the light and darkness are locked in intense conflict. Thank God for the angelic forces that fight off the works of darkness. Angels never minister selfishly; they serve so that all glory may be given to God as believers are strengthened. A classic example of the protective agency of angels is found in Acts 12:5-11.

As the scene opened, Peter lay bound in prison awaiting execution. James, the brother of John, had already been killed and there was little reason to suppose that Peter would escape the executioner's axe either. The magistrates intended to put him to death as a favor to those who opposed the gospel and the works of God. Surely the believers had prayed for James, but God had chosen to deliver him through death. Now the church was praying for Peter.

As he lay sleeping an angel appeared, not deterred by such things as doors or iron bars. The angel came into the prison cell, shook Peter awake and told him to prepare to escape. As a light shone in the prison the chains fell off Peter, and having dressed, he followed the angel out. Doors supernaturally opened because Peter could not pass through locked doors as the angel had. What a mighty deliverance God achieved through His angel!

Many experiences in both Old and New Testaments grew out of the imprisonment of God's saints, calling either for God to deliver directly, or to intervene through angels acting in His name. Many today who are captive in the chains of depression can take courage to believe in the prospect of deliverance. God has no favorites and declares that angels will minister to all the heirs of faith. If we, the sons of God, would only realize how close His ministering angels are, what calm assurance we could have in facing the cataclysms of life. While we do not place our faith directly in angels, we should place it in the God who rules the angels; then we can have peace.[3]

Jeannie handed the book back to Brother Raymond. He thought she was going to cry. Her eyes welled up with tears, but she surprised him by smiling. "That pretty much sums up what you've been trying to tell me," she said. "'The cataclysms of life...' It sounds like he was talking directly to me."

"He is," the minister said, "through God's Word. Anges Sanford, in her book, *The Healing Light*, gives several beautiful illustrations of our Heavenly Father's protection when one of His little ones learns to abide under the shadow of the Almighty. She writes:

> The reality of the circle of protection in which those who trust Him can walk was known even to men of the Old Testament. 'A thousand shall fall at thy side and ten thousand at thy right hand,' wrote the Psalmist. 'But it shall not come nigh thee.' And it didn't! Many of the young men of the parish told of miraculous instances of protection. They felt it. They knew it. 'Oh Lord, open his eyes that he may see,' prayed Elisha for his fearful manservant. And the Lord showed the manservant pictorially that reality of protection that Elisha had seen with the spiritual eye: He beheld the hills round about Elisha full of chariots of fire and horsemen of fire.
>
> A missionary once taught an ignorant Chinese woman that she was God's child. This new-born child of God stood at the railway station when a bombing raid began. She raised her oil paper umbrella. 'I am

God's child, so I can't be hurt!' she screamed to the crowd. 'Whoever gets under my umbrella with me will be safe.'

Four helpless ones crowded under the umbrella with God's child. When the raid was over, only these five stood alive and unharmed amid the shambles. Under the umbrella of the Almighty they had found their refuge until this tyranny was overpast.

A certain missionary traveled alone and unhurt among cannibal tribes. Years later he converted the chief of the tribes.

'I want to ask you something,' said the convert. 'Do you remember your first trip through this country?'

'I do indeed,' replied the missionary, who had been conscious on that dangerous trip of hostile, unseen presences, of following footsteps.

'Who were those two shining ones who walked on either side of you?' the chieftain asked.

Nor is it given only to a cannibal chieftain to see the gardian angels of the Lord. My father-in-law once walked at night through a lonely wood, followed by a man who hated him. Years later upon his death-bed the man made a confession to the once-hated priest. 'I planned to kill you that night,' he said.

'Why didn't you do it?' asked my father-in-law.

'How could I, sir,' asked the man, surprised, 'when I saw a strong man walking on either side of you?'

To both of these men the protection of God was made pictorially, in terms of presence and light.[4]

"In my final illustration, Agnes Sanford shows us how we may walk in the protection of our Heavenly Father's light. For He is the Father of light with whom is no variableness. In *The Healing Light*, she tells how pilots saw a circle of light on the ocean and assumed that a man in danger must be calling for help with his flashlight. Instead of a man on a raft, they found a man holding onto a piece of wood. It was God's circle of light that had directed them to that man.''[5]

Jeannie glanced at her watch, perceiving with shock that she had spent most of the afternoon listening to Brother Raymond.

"This has been a fantastic conversation," she said, smiling. "It's still difficult for me to grasp the entire scope of it intellectually, yet I know what a mess our lives are in. I'm willing to accept what you say on faith."

Brother Raymond nodded. "That's the beginning of wisdom and humility."

"Brother Raymond, I would like to receive the baptism of the Holy Spirit."

"Of course. As an act of faith, will you renounce all involvement with the occult?"

"I will. And I confess that I've believed in the doctrine of reincarnation. I have followed horoscopes daily, and aided my husband in charting astrological signs. I've been involved with automatic writing and the ouija board, and I've sought fortunetellers.

"I renounce all connections with all these evil practices in which I have indulged.

"Lord, I'm genuinely sorry that I did these things which I now know to be an abomination to You, and I promise that I will never do any of them again. Please forgive all of them, in Jesus' name!"

The old minister spoke softly. "Jesus Christ has just forgiven your sins because His Word says in 1 John 1:9, 'If we confess our sins, he is faithful and just to forgive us our sins, and to cleanse us from all unrighteousness.' Do you know, Jeannie, that Jesus is your personal Savior? Have you accepted Him as your Savior and Lord."

"Yes, I met Him today in the quietness of the chapel."

"Now, Jeannie, meet Him as your baptizer with the Holy Spirit."

Gently Brother Raymond laid his hands on her head and said, "Jesus, please baptize her with the Holy Spirit." Then he began praising God, first in English, and then in a language of the spirit. It was so beautiful and as he prayed in this heavenly language, Jeannie's heart became filled with a marvelous light that crowded out the darkness of fear, doubt and torment. A peace enveloped her that transcended all her understanding.

Sounds which she was not thinking began forming in her mind and before she realized it, she was speaking in a language she didn't understand. She didn't know what she was saying, but she knew her heart was filled with love for God. Her search had ended.

"This is a gift from God, freely given," Brother Raymond said softly. "Freely accept His love. Remember that this gift of the Holy Spirit is a gift and its effectiveness depends on how you use it. If a friend gave you a beautiful piano, and you let it gather dust, it would be of little value to you. But if you played beautiful music on it daily, it would be a blessing to you and to others who listened. Even having King Solomon as a friend would be a waste unless you followed his advice. Pray many times every day in your new heavenly spirit language."

"Brother Raymond, I know that you are a very busy man, and that I've taken up most of your day. I don't know how to thank you."

She looked at his placid face, and his smile

refreshed her spirit. She knew instinctively that he practiced what he taught.

"Time is relative to God, Jeannie. I try to yield to Him. The act of complete dependence on the Lord is not easy for us humans, and it requires daily mental exercise. You've seen how many people find momentary peace by worshipping false gods. Imagine the power unleashed to the yielded vessel who meditates day and night on God's law. If you'll follow a few of the disciplinary laws commanded by our Lord, you'll find new life for yourself and freedom for others."

"I don't think I understand what you mean. Isn't just knowing Him sufficient?"

"I can see the manifestation of His presence all around you. You've emerged washed and regenerated into new life. But there's a deeper walk, and if you would find release for your husband, you must practice the truths Jesus taught. For example, He taught us to forgive."

The expression on Jeannie's face was one of anger and hurt. "You've really lost me this time." She walked to the window and looked out at the rain. "My wounds are too fresh and deep to forgive." Jeannie turned to him, her eyes brimming with tears. "Even if I forgave Barry, how could I ever forgive Carolyn? I've been hurt so deeply. It's impossible for me to forgive that woman."

Brother Raymond irritated her further by smiling in his slow, droll way. He surprised her by saying, "Yes, Jeannie, it is impossible for *you* to forgive them. But God said that things impossible for man are possible with Him. You have a helper within you now, the Holy Spirit. *God is love. Love is God. And love is in you*. The Holy Spirit, who has sealed you and is perfecting you until the day of Christ, can love and forgive. He only requires that you give the problem to Him. So I'm asking you to forgive them and then pray for them. Don't pray as an act of piety or duty, but pray believing that God will supply real compassion in your heart for them. By God's eternal law of sowing and reaping, you'll sow the peace that passeth all understanding in your heart, and God will cover them with a blanket of purity and love.''

"But, Brother Raymond, you haven't seen the pathetic state he's in. How can I dare to have hope?''

He walked over to her and took her hands in his. She looked down at the long fingers, and she felt the warmth and strength of those gentle hands that patiently turned the pages of God's Word every day of his life. She gazed into eyes that had known sorrow long ago and now knew only profound joy.

His voice was gently. "Always remember this, Jeannie — 'where sin abounds, grace doth much more abound.' "

A leaping response within her witnessed to his words, and gave her the faith to believe and to face the inevitable future.

And take the helmet of salvation, and the sword of the Spirit, which is the word of God.

Ephesians 6:17 NASB

19
FIGHT TO THE FINISH

Jeannie's gentle embrace told Loretta all she needed to know. She rejoiced inwardly with the angels that her friend was a fellow citizen in the household of God.

"Thanks for being such a special friend, Loretta. I appreciate the way you took the children, no questions asked."

"It's my pleasure. I picked them up about ten from the neighbors. They had a good time. But please don't keep me in suspense. I know you have a lot to tell me. I see you're loaded down with books. It looks like you're planning to start your own mobile library."

Jeannie laughed. "Brother Raymond was more than generous in his sharing of books. I think I brought half his library with me."

Jeannie told Loretta her story, savoring and reliving every part of the day as she told it.

Loretta felt relieved. She watched Jeannie's face as she talked, and noticed for the first time that Jeannie was really a beautiful woman, especially when she smiled. She looked tired and she had lost weight in the last few months, but she seemed happier than Loretta had ever seen her.

Jeannie cried when she told Loretta about her baptism with the Holy Spirit, then laughed heartily through her tears. "I sang in my new spirit language in the car at the top of my lungs all the way over here.

I realized how singing in the spirit edified me, lifting me out of the depression Satan had tricked me into."

Loretta laughed. "I dance a lot since I've been baptized with the Holy Spirit," she said. "With the vacuum cleaner, the broom, the mop. How do you think I lost all that weight?"

They burst out laughing. Loretta laughed so hard she fell out of her chair, which made them laugh even harder. Lucy and Michael ran into the room and when they saw their mother lying on the floor they ran over and jumped on her. She grabbed them and pulled them down on the floor and kissed them.

Jeannie stood up, wiping away the tears that were streaming down her face. She glanced at her watch. "I've been here an hour! What in the world have you done with my kids to keep them so quiet?"

Loretta stared at her, uncomprehending. "Jeannie, I thought you knew! Barry came for them hours ago. He didn't stay long, in fact he left his car running. He said you were tied up and couldn't come get them."

Jeannie was already dialing her home number, but it rang relentlessly. *It must be a hollow sound*, she thought, *a phone ringing in a house with no furnishings or sounds of playing children.*

She and Loretta jumped into her car, making the six-block drive to her house quickly. No one was home.

The sky was darkening fast as rain began to fall in huge drops on the windshield. "Jeannie, don't drive so fast," Loretta said, as they headed for Carolyn's house. "A speeding ticket won't help things right now."

"It's been a long time since Judy and I last made

this trip to Carolyn's," Jeannie said, ignoring Loretta's warning. "I've been tempted to go back, but I couldn't. One year, Loretta. One lousy year of my life wasted. A whole lifetime lived and wrecked in that short span of time. I can still hear Brother Raymond's words echoing in my mind." Tears ran down her face. "I can see his gentle eyes and his calm, easy manner. I can still hear him talking about love. He sat there and told me that the royal law in the scriptures is to love your neighbor as yourself. Love. Love. I can grasp it in a general way, but to love a person who has taken my husband and now my children... how am I supposed to do that?"

"You can't, Jeannie. But God in you can."

Still not comprehending that a two-way conversation existed, Jeannie rambled on.

"Was it actually just today that I talked with him? Am I already faced with an incredible testing? Am I supposed to smile and face up to that woman like a saint? Jesus was tested after His baptism when He was led by the Spirit into the wilderness. But I'm not that strong!"

"Jesus handled His testing by quoting scripture to Satan," Loretta said quietly. But she knew that her words fell on deaf ears. Jeannie was staring straight ahead, not seeing the road.

The house had seemed remote and strange the first time Jeannie had been there, but now it stood defiant and hostile. The brink of night revealed dimly lit windows. The sight of Barry's car parked under a huge oak tree caused a further tightening in her chest. She was sure she could hear her heart beating loudly.

A loud clap of thunder made them both jump.

The branches of the ancient trees were swept low by the harsh winds and the rain began to beat loudly on the roof of the car.

Jeannie jumped out of the car and the wind jerked the door out of her hands. She ran toward the gate, not realizing that she was sobbing heavily. Her only thought was to get to Mary and Charles, to get them away from that woman who might be telling them unknown or frightening things. She thought she heard Loretta cry out, but she ran on. As her hand boldly pressed the latch on the gate, she was startled by a sudden, sharp explosive sound just a few inches from her head. In her confusion she threw her arms over her head, thinking that lightening had struck an object next to her. Then she saw her. Carolyn was standing on the front porch, her long black hair whipping around her head and a vicious sneer on her face. *She was holding a gun!*

"I won't miss next time!" she screamed at Jeannie.

Jeannie stared at the gun with disbelief. She suddenly felt faint from the realization that Carolyn hated her enough to kill her. She could hear Loretta pleading with her to return to the car. But she couldn't leave, not now, not when her whole future was at stake. She couldn't lose everything to this woman. She wanted her husband and her children... *where were the children?*

She began to walk slowly toward Carolyn, then faltered in her steps. Nausea swept over her as she saw the figure standing in the dark behind Carolyn. She stared at him, unable to move for fear she would fall. It was Barry. Barry was standing behind this woman, hiding behind her skirts!

He stared back at her, then lowered his eyes and turned and walked into the house. Jeannie's eyes followed him as he walked in, then she looked back at Carolyn.

"I won't leave!" she cried, her eyes flashing with an uncontrollable anger. "I want to speak to my husband, and I demand to see my children! How dare you..." She suddenly caught a glimpse of Mary and Charles through the window. They were romping through the house, oblivious to the night's drama. And suddenly everything seemed so unreal — the children and Barry in this strange house, the gun Carolyn was holding. She was soaking wet now, and she began to shiver uncontrollably.

Carolyn raised the gun once more, her face distorted with hate. Obscenities rushed out of her mouth.

Jeannie feared for her life now. She wanted to run but her feet felt like they were rooted to the ground. She opened her mouth to cry out for help, but no sound came forth. She couldn't pull her eyes away from Carolyn's face. It was twisted and Carolyn's eyes were flashing with hatred. Jeannie flinched as she felt Loretta's hand on her arm.

"Remember this afternoon, Jeannie. Don't you realize what's happening?"

Jeannie didn't respond verbally, but she walked stiffly as she allowed Loretta to lead her gently back to the car.

She looked back as she got into the car. Carolyn was walking into the house. She put her head back on the seat and closed her eyes. They sat in silence for a few minutes.

Jeannie finally spoke. "Have I failed already?"

"No, honey. You haven't failed. You've just learned a very valuable lesson in the Spirit-filled walk. The Holy Spirit is with you to help, but He won't push His presence or His advice on you. Just as you came to Him for salvation with nothing to offer but yourself, you face each day and each problem the same way. You can do nothing to *earn* salvation or love. He's already paid the price. But you can offer Him yourself and your willingness to yield and obey His will."

Jeannie felt as though she was being pushed and pulled in a cruel game of tug-o-war. She wanted Barry and the children back — that was foremost. She couldn't be expected to live without them! She began sobbing heavily again. She felt as though her grief was too much to bear. Barry wouldn't come back to her! He had stood in the shadows and watched Carolyn almost kill her!

The story of Job suddenly flashed through her mind. She knew now how he had felt when he lost his family and all his material possessions. She knew his sorrow and his will to die. The world had come crashing down on his head too. Oh, that God would appear to her as He had to Job and tell her what she had done to deserve this. God had sent poisoned arrows through her heart, just as He had sent them through Job's.

She looked up suddenly and caught her breath. It wasn't God who had hurt Job; it was Satan. Wasn't it? Satan had brought sorrow to Job, not God. God had only allowed it to happen to test Job's faith. Job had doubted God's providence, just as she had, but then he had repented in dust and ashes, and God had restored his wealth and happiness!

She had seen the power of God today — she knew at the moment of baptism that He could fight her battles for her with strength far greater than all the armies of the world put together. Brother Raymond had told her that her grief and anger gave a foothold to Satan. Ephesians 6 promised that if she put on all of God's armor she would be able to stand safe against Satan's strategies and tricks. She knew now that she was fighting the unseen world the gentle old minister had spoken of. Paul warns us to use every piece of God's armor to resist the enemy whenever he attacks and when it is all over, we will be standing up; and to do this, he said, we need the strong belt of truth and the breastplate of God's approval, faith as our shield to stop the fiery arrows aimed at us by Satan, the helmet of salvation and the sword of the Spirit — which is the Word of God.

Jeannie raised her arms. "Father, forgive me." She spoke softly. "Forgive me for trying to handle this situation myself. Forgive me for not leaning on Your understanding. Father, I have heard splendid accounts about Your supernatural love for Your children. I thank You that I am Your child. And I thank You that You are handling this situation for me. Amen."

Was it mere coincidence that the rain began to subside? The two friends sat very quietly in God's still assurance. Then they heard Carolyn's bellowing voice once more, and they saw her walking toward the car, still holding the gun. But this time she did not hold the gun in a shooting position.

"Come get him!" she yelled. "Come get your brats, too. I have no use for him anymore. He's less than a man, hiding behind my skirt, wanting me to make all the major decisions. I don't see how a man like him could help my cause. Or your children, either! They're just as weak as their father!''

Jeannie walked quickly past Carolyn into the house. She saw why Barry hadn't come out on his own. He sat in a chair with a twisted smile on his face.

Mary and Charles ran in to greet their mother, excitedly relating the day's activities to her.

''We went to a graveyard!'' Charles said. ''And a funny man was there wearing a robe. And he kept saying a poem over and over.''

''And we got to hand out freedom tracts to people,'' said Mary, proud that she had learned new words. Loretta led the children out of the room.

Jeannie took Barry's hand, and he followed her as obediently as the children.

''Come on, Barry,'' she said. ''We're going home.''

Therefore, my beloved brethren, be steadfast, immovable, always abounding in the work of the Lord, knowing that your toil is not in vain in the Lord.

1 Corinthians 15:58

20
LIFE AND LOVE AT LAST

Jeannie knelt in the quietness of morning, completely dependent upon the ministering of the Holy Spirit. Each day as she prayed softly in her new language, all her inner hostilities would leave, and in their place an inner peace would triumph. She knew that God had promised peace like the world never knows. He promised in Isaiah 43:2 of *The Living Bible* that He would be with her when she passed through deep waters and great trouble, and He promised that when she went through the rivers of difficulties, she would not drown; and He even promised that His followers would not be burned up when they walked through the fire of oppression.

She marveled at the peace and joy that penetrated her whole being. She had passed through many deep waters and fires during the past year. Her personality had blossomed as she yielded daily to Christ's love and laws. The love and wisdom of her divine teacher guided each step. She knew now that Jesus was the most profound psychiatrist and the greatest physician. She had tapped the source and received the healing balm of Gilead.

He fulfilled His promise in Proverbs to bring health to the whole man and healing to the nerves. Whenever a root of bitterness began to creep into her soul, she followed the Lord's commandment to love her enemies. Whenever resentment and jealousy toward Barry or Carolyn raised their serpent heads, she prayed for them. And, according to God's divine law, the peace that passeth all understanding always followed the knowledge that she was God's child and had inherent rights to all spiritual blessings.

She found a hiding place in Jesus, and her mind, body, and soul received the purging by the living Word and the living water. She rejoiced with the psalmist that God was causing her to be "like a tree planted by the rivers of water, that bringeth forth his fruit in his season," according to Psalm 1:3. An abiding faith in Barry's restoration was planted deep within her.

She could see no external results of the fruit of faith in Barry's life, but she held a mental picture of him firmly in her mind, a picture of the future Barry. She saw an older, more mature man than the one she had met on campus years ago. But her image of him still possessed boyish qualities and vulnerabilities. Restored in her heart and mind was the one who loved her, much wiser now, with all his ambitions and dreams channeled in the flow of God's love.

She knew that she could not have taken Barry back without Jesus. She could never have forgiven him for his weaknesses and taken him home with her that horrible night if God hadn't washed away her bitterness. She loved Barry now more than ever, because she could now look at him through the eyes of Jesus, with a love that wasn't affected by the things around her.

She remembered how complicated occultic meditation had been, and she compared that with her morning meditations now, which were as versatile and free as the Holy Spirit Himself. She sometimes dwelt on God's Word in the garden, quietly sipping a cup of coffee. She no longer needed the wine she used to drink — she had the new wine — the Holy Spirit now. As she enjoyed her coffee, she saw the dew gently pressing the tiny folds of the rose; the magnificent stems of the palm reaching heavenward, exposing strips of the blue sky; the mockingbird singing high on the pine above her; and the woodpecker pecking nearby, undisturbed by her presence. Other times she knelt by her bed allowing the One who said He is the Vine to fill her with His love. The thoughts caused her to smile. She could praise the Lord sitting down, standing up, kneeling, washing clothes, peeling potatoes, or standing on her head. Every heartbeat within her praised Him, and He rewarded her with joy unspeakable and full of glory.

Jeannie drank her usual small glass of orange juice for breakfast. Her lunch would consist of a small salad, and her evening meal would be light, a small portion of fruit and yogurt. She claimed the promise of Isaiah — that her fasting would loose the bonds of wickedness, undo the bands of the yoke, and let her oppressed loved one go free.

Barry's behavior did not show any visible changes. He walked into the kitchen, poured a drink, and walked by her without recognition. But Jeannie was faithful. She knew that God could heal Barry's wounds just as he has put a "Band-Aid" on Charles' little heartaches. The days passed into months while Jeannie ministered to a totally unresponsive husband. But she was not shaken by his lack of response. She knew that faith was the assurance of the thing she hoped for: the total healing of her husband.

Sometimes he would respond unexpectedly, but

it was always a harsh response, a lashing out at her wholesomeness. This personage with the body and face of her husband would speak to her with an alien voice, tormenting her.

"You are less than a woman," he would say. "You should be more like Carolyn. You spend your whole day cooking, cleaning, and sewing, acting as though you enjoy it. I don't believe any of it. I don't know what your game is, but I know it's not like you. You always have a silly smile on your face. Trying to maintain a contented facade! It disgusts me!"

Weeks of silence and oblivion to her presence always preceded another torrent of angry words and accusations. He always compared her unfavorably with Carolyn. She wondered if Barry was totally blocking out the fact that Carolyn had banished him from her life. He seemed to be living on memories of her.

"Carolyn has a remedy that would solve all our problems," Barry would say. "She thinks that all people should live together peacefully without quarreling or bickering. Her philosophy and wisdom are eons ahead of our present society. According to Carolyn, the three of us could even live together in harmony. You could continue in your role as nurse, if you could continue your act that long."

At these moments Jeannie would feel anger, jealousy, self-pity, and resentment. If she nurtured those feelings, bitterness would root within her and poison her attitude. She knew the importance of thinking on things above, not on things of the world around her. The apostle Paul had said, "Think about things that are pure and lovely, and dwell on the fine, good things in others" (Philippians 4:8 *TLB*). She was training her mind to think thoughts of life, love, and grace in Jesus. She would think of all of the good things that Barry had accomplished in the past, and then she would think happily of the person he was going to be in Christ. She would not allow the wars in the thinking realm to rob her of peace and her rightful status in Christ. She would then hear the calm voice of Brother Raymond. "If you have the greatest and wisest friend in all the world and you do not follow or seek his counsel, the friendship means nothing." And she would slip quietly into her room and solicit His advice.

Gradually the anger and harsh verbal beating from Barry subsided, and they were replaced by his withdrawn, almost catatonic personality.

He favored sitting in the old rocking chair on the back patio. He rocked endlessly and listlessly, staring into space. She fed him like a child. He wore the clothes she picked out for him, and he obeyed the bedtime curfew as obediently as Mary and Charles.

Jeannie read the scripture, "Faith is the substance of things hoped for, the evidence of things not seen." Her faith would start to diminish as she cared for an ungrateful, unresponsive husband. Then she would remember that the carnal mind is enmity against God. She knew that she would meet defeat if she looked at the situation through natural eyes. The book of Hebrews claimed that without faith it is impossible to please Him, and her whole being yearned to please the Master who had set her free.

A year had passed since the night she had brought Barry home. Autumn leaves began to fall. Jeannie spent her days praying and fasting. Friends no longer called. Carolyn had long since disappeared from the scene, having no sympathy for the weakened man she had thrown back at Jeannie. Loretta had come a few times, but she finally told Jeannie that she felt she should stay away until things got better.

Barry sat alone on the patio, rocking and staring straight ahead. His eyes blinked in flickering awareness of the falling leaves, the arrival of the butterflies, bees, and hummingbirds that danced with amazing precision among the flaming red bottlebrushes. The warmth of the sun which blended with the tinge of cool that fall brings gave an awakening sensation to his taut muscles. He looked down at his arms and realized that they were not tan from the summer as they usually were at this time of year. He thought of Jeannie, sitting alone in the kitchen with no one to talk to, and for a moment he yearned to go to her and say something to make her laugh again.

He knew she was peaceful somehow, and happy at times, but she was lonely for him and his heart went out to her.

The past year had been fruitless. He could think of nothing he had accomplished that was worthwhile. He thought of Carolyn for an instant, then tried to block out the sight of her. The Carolyn he remembered held a gun, and she was screaming ugly things at a frightened Jeannie.

"I was so blind," he said out loud.

He was suddenly aware of a companion rocking in a nearby chair in rhythm with his own movements. He looked up, startled, and saw that it was an old man — a very poor old man, from the looks of his clothes.

"Who are you?" Barry asked him, standing up.

"Where's Jeannie?"

Barry sensed that his companion was friendly. His presence furnished the same warm sensation that the sun supplied to Barry's body, thawing his tired spirit and regenerating it with life. Barry was relieved to see that the man was not a member of the affluent congregation that had rejected him. He knew this as he surveyed the tattered brown coat and the prominent hole in one of his shoes.

Barry's eyes glided over the shoes and the brown coat, and into the face, where he met friendly, caring eyes.

"God loves you," the old man said simply.

"People don't love me," Barry said, looking away. "I've betrayed them. I have no one now. No one."

"God loves you. He is love."

"Even after..."

"Yes. Even after. He loves you."

Barry was reminded of words he had once shallowly spoken: "Have faith in God." Suddenly, he was acutely aware of how much faith God must have had in man to give him freedom of choice. He realized how many wrong choices man had made. Yet God's forgiveness was ever available, and God had faith that man would choose Him as the ultimate choice and the only reality. Jesus was the end result in the pursuit of truth.

Then Barry thought of his own wrong choices, of all the heartache he had caused because of his mistakes. Yet somehow he knew that God was not condemning him for them, but that He still loved him and stood ready to forgive.

Overwhelmed by God's love for him and his

freedom of choice, Barry knelt by the chair in submission and prayed.

Barry startled Jeannie by entering the kitchen where she sat. He rarely left his chair unless he was coached. She turned and faced him.

His face seemed older, wiser somehow. But she saw a glimpse of the impulsive, ambitious, gentle young man she had met in that campus parlor years before.

He spoke the words she had yearned to hear. "You know, lately you seem like my old girl again."

She ran to him and flung her arms around his neck. He pulled her close to him and buried his face in her hair.

They were too involved in their embrace to see the old man walk away, an old man unaffected by time, an old man whose destiny it was to serve.

NOTES

CHAPTER FIFTEEN

1. Billy Graham, *Angels: God's Secret Agents*. (New York: Doubleday & Company, Inc., 1975), p. 63.
2. Gordon Lindsay, *Sorcery in America* pamphlet series. (Dallas, Texas: Christ For The Nations, 1973).
3. *Sorcery in America*, Vol. II, p. 31.
4. *Sorcery in America*, Vol. II, pp. 31-32.
5. *Sorcery in America*, Vol. II, p. 32.
6. *Sorcery in America*, Vol. II, pp. 3-7.
7. *Sorcery in America*, Vol. II, pp. 5-6.

CHAPTER SEVENTEEN

1. *Sorcery in America*, Vol. II, p. 17.
2. *Sorcery in America*, Vol. II, p. 23.
3. *Sorcery in America*, Vol. II, pp. 9-10.
4. Agnes Sanford, *Sealed Orders*. (Plainfield, N.J.: Logos International, 1972), p. 14.

CHAPTER EIGHTEEN

1. *Angels: God's Secret Agents*, pp. 1-4.
2. Corrie ten Boom as quoted in *Angels: God's Secret Agents*, pp. 90-91.
3. *Angels: God's Secret Agents*, pp. 94-95.
4. Agnes Sanford, *The Healing Light*. (Plainfield, N.J.: Logos International, 1974), pp. 173-174.
5. *The Healing Light*, p. 175.

Georgeanne and Roger DeWitt are both Bible teachers and ministers. Their first pastorate was of a United Methodist Church in 1977. Today they are pastors of New Covenant Praise, a rapidly growing church in Houston, Texas.

Georgeanne's most inspired teaching is on casting down imaginations. She has seen captives set free by the preaching of God's Word. She is an intercessor who has been used by the Lord to administer healing and word of knowledge. The Lord uses her to minister to the bodies and minds of those people she has counseled.

Roger excels in teaching on praise and worship and exhorts his listeners at church and on a daily radio broadcast. Georgeanne has testified in *Women's Aglow* groups and Roger has spoken in *Full Gospel Business Men's Fellowships*, Bible studies and churches.

The DeWitts have two daughters. Their older daughter, Katherine, has one son, Shane, and identical twin daughters, Lisa and Laura. Their younger daughter, Jennifer, graduated with a degree in commercial art from Oral Roberts University and is an active witness for the Lord. She is married to D. Hal Hubbard. They have one son, David Allen.

To contact Georgeanne DeWitt,
write:

DeWitt Ministries
P. O. Box 73306
Houston, Texas 77273-3306

*Please include your prayer requests
and comments when you write.*

Additional copies of
Rescue From the Dark Side
are available from your local bookstore,
or from:

P. O. Box 35035
Tulsa, Oklahoma 74153